'JUST PLAY NATURALLY'

'JUST PLAY NATURALLY'

VIVIEN MACKIE

In Conversation With
JOE ARMSTRONG

An account of her cello study
with Pablo Casals in the 1950's
and her discovery of the resonance between
his teaching and the principles of the Alexander Technique

BOSTON–LONDON   1984–2000

DUENDE EDITIONS

ISBN: 0-9717004-0-0

Production & Design: Robert B. Smyth

Photgraph of F.M. Alexander © 2000 The Society of Teachers
of the Alexander Technique, London

Photograph of Pablo Casals
No Source Found
With Consent of Butterworth-Heinemann, Oxford, England

ACKNOWLEDGMENTS

We wish to express our gratitude to all those who have helped in the process of writing this book and encouraged us by their support and excitement about the subject. They include, for their help in transcribing, Karen Mansur Carter and Jessica Stensrud. And for their encouragement or for reading parts or all of the manuscript, Walter Carrington, Larry Carter, Ann Carter, Mary Alice McCann, Ann Gabhart, Mowry Pearson, Peter Davison, Rev. Eulalio Luna, Mark Latham, Jeffrey Mitchell, Patricia Murray, Rosanna Warren, Rika Lesser, Margaret Cheng Tuttle, Lucile Newman, Beret Arcaya, S. Vreni of Grandchamp, Maureen Thomas, John Lorne Campbell, and his wife Margaret Fay Shaw.

JOE ARMSTRONG
VIVIEN MACKIE

TO OUR TEACHERS

TABLE OF CONTENTS

FOREWORD

When I left England for my ten lessons with Casals, I was, after all, just 'going abroad for a year's polish' to round off quite a successful career so far, so I more or less *glided* into Prades as a smooth continuance of my musical life. I knew it would be an adventure, but when you arrive at the railway station in Prades you are immediately in the presence of Mount Canigou, two and a half times the height of Britain's highest mountain and in far more rugged country than I could have imagined—and that gave me just an inkling of the ruggedness and grandeur of what lay ahead. I would never have guessed then that I was going to stay three years in this wonderful place.

Over the years since I was there in the 1950's, the idea of writing a book about my time with Casals has flitted about like a moth at the back of my mind, sometimes disappearing for years at a time, and then flickering back into view.

Two things held me back. The first big stumbling-block, which I came to very early on when I made a first attempt for a student magazine, was that it seemed impossible to write about Casals' revolutionary and revelatory teaching without appearing to denigrate everything about my earlier musical training. So much that he said and did was *contrary* to what had gone before. A few decades later, as a teacher myself, I know more about teaching and learning, and how complex a matter it all is. I've even enjoyed hearing myself contradict myself.

The second daunting thought was that you must have special gifts to be able to write a book. I wanted to weave among the story of the lessons an account of my forays into the formidable country to find a remote abandoned village, or a cave, or an ancient watchtower—an arduous pastime that provided a necessary counter-balance to the intensity of the cello work. There should have been illustrations, too, by my own hand.

Then in 1970, when the moth had been out of sight for some time, I met Joe on our Alexander teacher training course, and we began to talk endlessly about music and Casals, and I began to teach Joe cello. His questions and almost daily 'discoveries' as he practised the cello opened up all kinds of backwaters; he made me go exploring in my experience in a way I found quite thrilling. And then we began to think:perhaps this is going to be the book I wanted to write. And here it is. The illustrations never happened, nor the accounts of the rambles—but just as the Alexander experience has flooded continuously in and out of the musical, so I know the essence of the whole experience of living in Prades is in there too.

VIVEN MACKIE
London
May 2000

INTRODUCTION

In 1970, toward the end of my first year of training to become a teacher of the Alexander Technique,[1] I heard that Vivien Mackie, a professional cellist who had studied extensively with Pablo Casals, was going to join the class too. Since I had come to revere and respect Casals as the greatest musician of our time, the prospect of getting to know and maybe even work closely with someone who possessed something of his understanding and approach to music was beyond anything I could have hoped for at that stage of my musical career.

Before enrolling in the three-year Alexander teacher's course given in London by Walter Carrington, his wife Dilys, and Peggy Williams, I'd already earned a bachelor's degree in music, played flute for three years

---

[1] The Alexander Technique is a method for transmitting through a teacher's hands the experience of an integrated working of a person's postural mechanisms in relation to gravity. It also involves learning how to maintain this integration in every aspect of living. The technique was developed over a hundred years ago by F. Matthias Alexander and is now taught worldwide. Alexander wrote four books on his work, *Man's Supreme Inheritance*, *Constructive Conscious Control of the Individual*, *The Use of the Self*, and *The Universal Constant in Living*. For a detailed description of the use of the technique by musicians, see the Appendix article by Vivien Mackie, 'The Alexander Technique and the Professional Musician.'

in an American military concert band, and had seen from several years of lessons in the Alexander Technique how essential it would be for me as a performer to achieve the fully integrated 'use of my self' that is the Technique's goal. I was also convinced that being able to impart the experience of that integration to others would be invaluable to whatever teaching I might do as a professional musician. By the time Vivien started the course I had also met a number of excellent professional musicians who'd been drawn to the Alexander teacher training for the same reasons I had, and I was very impressed by their accomplishment and brilliance. Yet I felt that establishing a connection with her could lead into a deeper realm of experience and knowledge that I was still thirsting and searching for but whose contents I had only vaguely guessed at

Up to then I had also spent a lot of time listening to many recordings of Casals playing, conducting, and teaching, as well as reading as much as I could about his ideas on music and life in various books like *Conversations with Casals* and *Joys and Sorrows*. And just before going to England I'd even had the chance to see him in person at one of the famous master classes he taught at the Marlboro Music Festival in Vermont, which certainly confirmed my conviction about his greatness. The young professional cellist who performed for him in the class that day was obviously transformed completely by it, and it seemed like the same 'magical' thing had happened to her that I had experienced in lessons with my first teacher, the remarkable flutist Carl Petkoff; but she was clearly as mystified as I was about how it came about. My study with my flute teacher had been unexpectedly cut short, so I hadn't had the chance to find out if I could learn how to produce the magic consistently on my own; however, witnessing the transformation happen to this cellist right in Casals' presence made it seem even more tangible, simple, and pure—whatever 'it' was. I thought it must have had something to do with understanding the essential elements of 'musicality' and knew I wouldn't be content until I explored every avenue I could to find out what the 'secret' was and how it worked—if that was actually possible.

'Musicality' (as distinct from 'musicianship') was believed by most musicians I knew to be—like 'talent'—something innate. You supposedly either had it, or you didn't. Some felt it came in gradations, and I often heard colleagues and teachers saying, 'Oh, she's *so* musical!' Or '*very* musical!' Or '*not* a very musical player.' Others seemed to believe it could be brought out or developed as well as severely hampered—for instance, by nervousness and stage fright—or even lost or destroyed. But no one I knew could explain what musicality actually was or show what components, if any, made it up. In a way, it was almost taboo even to think of examining it in depth. (I still find this to be very much the case, some thirty years later, among the many professional musicians I work with.)

Teachers and conductors I'd had who seemed to take players *away* from musicality did it mainly, I thought, by the *way* they focused on technique and detail. One college flute teacher I had actually made me feel I'd lost my musicality completely for a while, until Alexander lessons rescued me from his divided approach. And since I'd seen from those experiences how malleable it could be, by the time I joined the Alexander teachers' course I'd already begun to wonder if musicality was something that could be better understood and maybe even taught—particularly with the aid of the Alexander Technique. Obviously, Casals was able to foster it superbly in his teaching and conducting—even when he was focusing on the simplest detail—maybe even *especially* then. But I doubted that I would ever have the chance to work with him directly to find out more about how he did it, since he was already well into his nineties by this time.

So before I even met Vivien, I knew I would try to question her as much as I could on every facet of her experience with Casals. As luck would have it, we seemed to be on the same wave-length right from our first meeting; and what's more, she actually seemed to be grateful—even somewhat relieved—to have the chance to talk about her work with Casals, because, to my surprise, I seemed to be the first person she knew who was really interested in hearing about every detail of it.

Also lucky for me, Vivien turned out to be a natural raconteur, and I began taking advantage of that by roping her into many long conversations—at lunch time in the garden at the Alexander school, on walks to and from our class through Kensington Gardens and Holland Park, and at her house over dinner with her delightful sons, James and Andrew. I was struck right off by her telling me how she too had lost touch with something precious in her playing by the time she'd left music school, and it had taken her intensive study with Casals to bring it back. It was soon clear that her experience with him was unique not only because of that, but also because she had worked with him longer than almost anyone else; so I felt even more that my questioning would begin to lead to the heart of what musicality is.

One evening after dinner I finally persuaded Vivien to play something for me, and everything that I might have expected to be present in her playing as a result of studying so extensively and comprehensively with

Casals was there—*and more*. She played an 'allemande' from one of the Bach unaccompanied cello suites, and I was overwhelmed by the power of life in it. All I could think to say was, 'Gosh! I didn't know a woman could play like that!' But then I quickly amended myself and said, 'I mean . . . I didn't know *anybody* could play like that!'

I realized then that, however illuminating our talks might be, they were probably only scratching the surface of what she had actually learned from her three whole years with Casals; so I decided to ask her if she would consider *teaching* me how to play the cello—thinking that it could be the most direct way of experiencing and understanding, at least 'second-hand,' the elements of how Casals had taught her that not only brought back what she had lost but also took her to the highest professional level. I also thought that it could be interesting for her, as a kind of experiment, to teach me, because my Alexander background coupled with my advanced musical experience might have something extra to offer her in what she was hoping to add to her cello teaching from the Alexander teacher training. She liked the idea very much, and, after we found a cello that I could keep at the school for my practicing and our lessons, we began 'doing cello' there together several times a week during our lunch breaks over the next year and a half or so.

I was amazed at what transpired in the lessons—especially compared to some instruction I'd had in a year of string class in music school. (I was actually supposed to be qualified to teach beginning strings merely by taking that course!) I'd hoped that because of this earlier experience I might be a little more receptive as a student, but I soon saw that none of that was even relevant to the way Vivien was teaching me. It was totally different from—even opposite to—what I thought most other string teachers were probably doing in their teaching, because she was getting me to experience a far broader range of expressive and kinaesthetic possibilities all over the instrument right from the start, by completely bypassing the conventional lengthy dwelling on the progression of distinctly confined left-hand positions. In a few months I was able to begin learning pieces I could never have conceived of playing at the end of my string course. And this difference in Vivien's approach only seems to me more pronounced today, after having had the chance both to work extensively with a large number of fine string players and teachers in my many years of Alexander teaching in Boston and to watch Vivien bring these revelations to most of *them* in Alexander string courses we've given here together.

During our Alexander training in England, Vivien and I also laid the groundwork for what would ultimately extend beyond our exchanges in my cello lessons into both a long-range teaching and performing collaboration and a close friendship. To be able to play chamber music with her, give Alexander music courses together, travel, and talk endlessly on so many aspects of music, Alexander teaching, and life in general is the greatest privilege.

As our collaboration developed and we probed further and further into the elements of musical expression, I could see that it would be very valuable to others if we could create some record of Vivien's experience with Casals and show how the elements of his great legacy can be understood and passed on especially with the aid of the Alexander Technique, since the process of learning and teaching it involves so many of the same understandings applied to life in general that Casals brought to cello teaching and all his music making. So in 1984 I suggested we start recording some of our conversations beginning by harking back to Vivien's initial study with him, continuing from there through her experience with the Alexander Technique, and then going on to her amalgamation of the two into her own unique way of teaching—not just cellists, but musicians of every kind— all around the world. She agreed, and this book is what came out of the project.

JOE ARMSTRONG
Boston, MA
February, 2000

I have heard what the talkers were talking, the talk
of the beginning and the end,
But I do not talk of the beginning or the end.

There was never any more inception than there is
now.

Nor any more youth or age than there is now,
And will never be any more perfection than there is
now.

Nor any more heaven or hell than there is now.

From 'Song of Myself'
Walt Whitman

I
BACKGROUND

Joe Armstrong: It think it would be a good idea to begin by saying something about Casals' background, since there might be some people reading this who don't know who he really was. It seems to me that there is a lot in the scope of what you have to say that could be just as valuable for non-musicians to read, because I think your experience with him was as unique in the realm of general living just as it was in music. So that knowing his background and what he did in his lifetime could be important for setting the stage.

Vivien Mackie: Yes.

JA. He was a great cellist—arguably the greatest. And even arguably the greatest musician of the 20th century. And he was also a great humanitarian. And a great teacher.

VM. Yes. All of that. Actually I didn't know a great deal about his history when I came to study the cello with him. I've learned later, for instance, that his father was organist and choirmaster in the little town near Barcelona where he was born.

JA. Didn't he skyrocket very early on in his career?

VM. Do you think he did? Well, of course, he was outstanding, but he certainly told me that he had some pretty bad notices from the critics, which doesn't suggest immediate wholesale success.

JA. Really? Then when would it have been that he became so famous? In the forties?

VM. Oh, long before then. Well, he was born in 1876. So by the time he was twenty or twenty-five he was on his way—and he had made his debut with the Lamoureux orchestra in Paris at twenty-two.

JA. So he had become an international figure soon after the turn of the century?

VM. Yes, I think so.

JA. At any rate, by the time you came to know Casals in the fifties, he was certainly a highly respected and great musician.

VM. Oh, goodness, yes.

JA. And by then he had already been in exile from Franco's dictatorship of Spain, living in the little town of Prades on the French side of the Pyrenees.

VM. Yes.

JA. And he had refused to perform again anywhere in the world until the dictatorship was removed from Spain; but then, at the anniversary of Bach's death, in 1950, some famous musicians from the U.S. persuaded him to let them come to Prades and start the great musical festivals that centered around him. And they also made many wonderful recordings of those performances—which are still available.

VM. Yes.

JA. How did you come to know about him then?

VM. I remember as a small child before the war hearing about him. His name was a household word in musical circles in Edinburgh. And then there was Madame Suggia, who was also a cellist we knew about, especially as she was painted by Augustus John, wearing that wonderful red dress. That *really* took my fancy!

JA. Pretty irresistible to a little girl! So you knew about Casals while you were growing up, but just as a 'name,' and one of the top cellists?

VM. Yes, but I wasn't particularly interested in cellists as such, as a youngster, because my world was bounded by my teacher, 'Auntie Ruth' [Ruth Waddell]. I remember asking my mother, when I was six or seven, 'Can I ever be as good as Auntie Ruth, do you think?'

JA. Then you had your wonderful cello teacher Olive Woodington at boarding school?

VM. Yes, and in 1947, while I was there, Casals came to play in London, and Olive suggested to the school authorities, whoever they were, that I might be allowed to go and hear him. But, one way and another, it just wasn't possible. I don't know whether that was because it was a particularly bad winter, and traveling was more difficult than usual. I think it was more probably that the school just couldn't, or wouldn't, see its way to letting me miss several classes. Or there was no one to escort me to London. So I never heard him until I was a music student at college,[1] and heard some of his Bach on a record. I thought it was pretty strange, and I didn't like it much. There had always been such a reverence for this great man, so his Bach was a surprise. I suppose I had expected something more congenial to my ear.

JA. Do you think that the main sense of reverence for him had come through Olive?

VM. No. As I said, Casals' name had been a household word. My mother played in the Reid Symphony Orchestra in Edinburgh, before I was born, and she used to talk about their conductor Sir Donald Francis Tovey, who was another great musician, and also a very great friend and admirer of Casals. (Casals often talked of him, too, while I was in Prades.) Tovey conducted the orchestra, and she played in it, and kept all the programmes. All the best soloists were invited to play with them, and of course Casals was one of those big names. My mother used to say how wonderful he was. So that was how I knew about him—but I wasn't

[1] The Royal College of Music, London

particularly interested at that age, before the War. Very, very early days in my life!

JA. And you still hadn't become very interested in him when you went to college in 1948?

VM. No. At boarding school we really didn't have the opportunity to listen to music much. The first Edinburgh International Festival was in 1947, and we grabbed the opportunity to go to hear all those wonderful players, but in fact, it wasn't until I got my traveling scholarship at the end of my four years in college that I began to consider the international music world in relation to *me*. At that time, just after the war, ordinary people weren't going to Europe much, so we were relatively isolated, and traveling abroad to study wasn't yet a general thing. So when I got my traveling scholarship, I might have traveled all the way to London, as some of the Scottish winners did! But I was already *in* London, so I looked to Europe.

JA. You needed to decide on some *place*?

VM. Some place, yes! My professor said, 'You must have learned French at school, so what about Paris? And didn't you learn Italian, too? Well then, what about Rome? Who teaches there?' I felt this was all wrong— if you have a precious scholarship, you don't choose a teacher for reasons like that! The only cellist I'd heard that I felt I might like to study with was André Navarra.

JA. Oh, really?

VM. Yes. But I felt very modest about studying with somebody 'big' at all. It was Olive Woodington who said, 'Well, my dear, there's Casals.' I said, 'Don't be silly.' But she pointed out that he could always say 'No.' And I thought, 'Well, I *have* got the college prize, and I've won a scholarship. Why should I suppose that the best is too good?' And since he could always say 'No,' some devil inside me rose to the challenge and said, 'O.K., Why not?' So I went to my cello professor and said, 'What about Casals?' And he said, 'Hmmm. You're flying high!' So I told him how I'd come to my decision, and he agreed to write to Casals on my behalf. So he did, and I suppose he said I seemed intelligent and worked hard, made lots of progress at college and so on. So Casals wrote me a postcard and said he would be pleased to see me on the 14th of October next.

JA. Ah, ha!

VM. And that's how I came to go!

JA. It's interesting that you hadn't thought anything like, 'Oh, I must go and find the greatest master if I'm going to achieve my fullest potential on the cello, and that must be Casals.

VM. Not at all, not at all. I was really very much lost, in spite of being particularly lucky in having two very fine professors at college, one for cello and one for piano. The cello professor, Ivor James, was especially fine in chamber music; so I'd had some very good background there. But nobody really knew much about what it was like outside England, and these professors didn't really have firsthand knowledge of the current professional scene.

JA. Because of the war?

VM. Not so much because of the war, but because they were professors in a college, you see?

JA. Oh.

VM. The cello professor played in a fine quartet, and my piano professor, Frank Merrick— a marvelous pianist, who was by then over seventy— specialised in some rather obscure composers. But their daily professional work was in college; so one didn't catch from them a very clear picture of what it was going to be like when you left their care. And you do rely on your teachers for the adumbrations of what you yourself are going to do. They made it quite clear to me that I was expected to be a soloist. And I had made it quite clear to them that being an orchestral player was not what I wanted. But I also said I was eager to teach— because I liked the idea of teaching. And they said, 'Oh, you're not going to have to do *that!*' which was very much to my surprise. I had always been told since I was a little girl, "You're a soloist, you know.' And since I went through all the competition festivals, winning all the cello classes I entered, and since I was invited to play on the radio at the age of eleven, I *did* seem to be a soloist. I remember skipping up the stairs at home when the invitation came from the BBC, thinking, 'I'm made! I've got there already! It's hard to get on the BBC!' you know?

JA. Yes!

VM. So, even though it was other people's idea that I was going to be a cellist, and a soloist, really from the start, I certainly had no feeling that

'I must put my talent in the care of someone great' or anything like that. I only knew I'd got this scholarship, and I'd better spend it somewhere, and spend it well, because I knew I had a lot of work to do.

JA. You'd got through college and you still didn't feel like you were at the point where you could embark on the career of being a soloist?

VM. No. Well, it was strange at college, because I was always sure that I wasn't going to do very well in the end of year exams, although I was undoubtedly one of the top two or three cellists who were in demand for chamber music all the way through. But I didn't expect to win the cello prize. I didn't dare to go and look at the list on the notice board. I thought my friend was pulling my leg when he told me I had; I couldn't believe it. I had no great opinion of myself, because I felt I was in a muddle, and yet I often turned up at the top of the list. Nobody else seemed to suspect that I was in a muddle.

JA. Why do you think you were in a muddle?

VM. I think because I had started very young and it all came very easily. My beloved first teacher and her sister, who taught the violin, were clever at finding talented youngsters, and I was one of them. I had a vivid imagination, and I loved the stories and pictures that came into my mind when I played. I saw lovely fairy-tale scenes, and so on and so forth. And it was rather dashing to win the classes in the competition festival in Edinburgh every year, ever younger for my class—so that one year the adjudicator (Ivor James, who was to be my professor when I went to college) rang his bell as I was on my way up to the platform and said, looking over the top of his glasses, 'Excuse me, are you quite sure you're under eighteen?' 'Yes, I'm eleven,' I squeaked, feeling very conspicuous with everybody's eyes on me. He loved that sort of joke.

JA. Ha, ha!

VM. So that all went very well and swimmingly, you see. And then almost immediately after came a dreadful time. I don't know what it was all about, but I believe it was just my own adolescence coming along. I ceased to be able to just sit down and play. I needed to know how to do it. Something in me was saying 'Yes, but HOW, but HOW?' My first teacher and my mother were unsympathetic to this and said, 'You've got to work harder.' Nobody understood! 'Working harder' didn't help, and for the first time I didn't win my class at the festival. I was making a great effort and getting nowhere, for the first time in my life, and it was a very unpleasant experience indeed. This was my very own self letting me down.

JA. Yes.

VM. So I think the muddle started then. When I went to Olive Woodington, for my first lesson at boarding school, when I was fourteen, she asked me what things I'd been doing recently, before I even played for her. I remember very clearly telling her about the BBC, and how I'd been preparing the pieces for a professional diploma, and giving her my credentials with one hand, as it were, and on the other hand turning away from those credentials, and feeling, 'I can't, I can't have done all those things.' I felt torn in two. Yet I *had* done all those things, and I had every right to present these achievements as representative of what I could do. Yet my deep and intense feeling about it was, 'But I can't.'

JA. Even at that age?

VM. At fourteen, yes. But Olive was a very clever woman, and she saw it all in a flash. She quickly turned round and pretended to be shuffling music or something, probably to save me embarrassment. Later she told me that dealing with me was like trying to get at a hedgehog. She said it was about a year before she felt she was beginning to unroll this hedgehog, and I don't know how she did it. She just waited until I uncurled, I think.

JA. And didn't she help you with the muddle a lot, because she was such a wonderful person and teacher?

VM. She helped me very greatly with the muddle; but I didn't know what the muddle was about, and she could only guess. She made some very, very good guesses.

JA. I see.

VM. She was deeply understanding. I know now that she thought there was a sizable talent there, and she could see that I was thoroughly messed up, but she didn't talk to me then about my 'sizable talent' or goad me in any way, you know. So in the three years that I was with her, I uncurled from this hedgehog condition and certainly made some progress, so that at the age of seventeen and the end of my schooldays, I was able to play two movements of the Haydn concerto in D with the school orchestra.

JA. Yes.

VM. In fact there was never any *pressure* from Olive to practice. She even said one day in my last year, 'I think we've had enough cello for today; let's go and have a coffee in town!' Quite unprecedented, and totally against the school rules. Olive really just calmed me down, put things back in perspective, and made me feel I could rely on her. She wasn't ambitious for me in the way that my first teacher had been.

JA. Yes.

VM. She let me catch up with myself. That's what she did.

JA. Can you remember anything specific she did in working with you cellistically that helped prepare you for college?

VM. I think, when I consider the early days of learning the cello, and how I got along by guesswork and on a pretty good ear, that she must have made me take responsibility for finding my way about the cello much more than I had done before. She certainly made me listen to myself a great deal more, and made me consider the business of performing, because this had become very difficult for me. Very difficult. When it came to playing to people it was like trying to lift the bow off and play at the same time. I tried to play and not to play all at the same time, in case it was going to be wrong, you know?

JA. Yes.

VM. A very uncomfortable situation. I don't know that I can remember ever enjoying playing the cello at school—in spite of Olive's deep friendship and support—as I enjoyed playing the piano, for instance, and singing, and composing. Those were all pleasure and delight.

JA. So her helping you to catch up with yourself somehow helped you make it through your college years in a way, perhaps, that you wouldn't have been able to otherwise?

VM. Oh, I think that's pretty well for certain. Or I would have been, as I think I was not, highly neurotic.

JA. Or one of those people who practise twelve hours a day.

VM. No, I was never one of those! I said to Olive once, 'I don't think I've got the guts to practise the required amount.' And she said, 'My dear, I think you've got the guts for anything.' And that kind of confidence in me was very nice—exhilarating and fortifying. Whereas my first teacher had been anxious for me to get on and have stuff to show for what I had done, and I had acquired a certain degree of superficial skill too young and for the wrong reasons. I think that when children start to learn an instrument very young along those lines, particularly if they're in a little pocket in a rather tucked-away place, there's a danger of becoming a big fish in a small pool, and in some ways they simply become overdeveloped, especially at a young age when they're developing fast. At least in those days. Perhaps now that there are so many more young people studying music, and worldwide communication is so much easier, the attitudes to teaching them are rather more enlightened. I should like to think so, but I'm afraid it's still going on.

JA. Yes, I think it is.

VM. Besides, it makes childhood so uncomfortable, if you're outstandingly good at something. It's very hard to be like the others. I wanted that more than anything—to fit in. So I think that catching-up time with Olive was terribly, terribly important for me.

JA. Then as you went on in college I suppose it became clearer and clearer that you were in a muddle?

VM. Well, not really. I was in no hurry to know I was in a muddle, and I would have tried very hard, I imagine, to convince myself that I was not in one, since my 'results' seemed to suggest that I wasn't. I think my unhappiness and unease at college was mostly social, as with so many of the students. After all, you come from all kinds of backgrounds and all kinds of levels of experience, and you suddenly have to be 'adult.' And what's more, you have to concentrate on music and learn to practise seriously on your own. It's a very big change that happens at that stage.

JA. You're dealing with all that new stuff.

VM. Dealing with all that new stuff as well. And then the quantity of work that the students were expected to get through was colossal. I was playing seven or eight hours a day, and really scrambling, as students still do, to meet the deadlines.

JA. You mean practising that much?

VM. Not practising as such. I took part in a great deal of chamber music—lots and lots of quartets, trios, and other interesting ensembles. There was a lot of music to get to know, and that part of it I loved, because I really did like learning new music—meeting the music. In fact I suppose it was the first time I had got to grips with the real repertoire, because, after all, as a schoolgirl, you're not touching on very much beyond 'exam pieces' and so on.

JA. No.

VM. The school orchestra's not capable of very much, and there aren't many quartets and trios that could have been learned in those days by many schoolchildren, so College was my first exposure to a lot of music, and I loved it. You see we didn't have the radio and recordings on the scale we have now. So that part—learning the new music—was all very good. I think I just chose not to get over-anxious about the muddle—and besides, I was too busy to think much about it.

JA. So even by the end of college you weren't thinking, 'Oh, now I've got to get busy and find my way out of the muddle.' You were just going to go and study abroad.

VM. Yes. The professors said, 'A year's polish.' 'A year abroad, and you will be polished.' It didn't seem to matter much to whom I went.

JA. So Casals accepted you, and you went to study with him the next autumn. That was 1952?

VM. Yes! That was 1952.

II

FIRST LESSONS WITH CASALS

JA. And when you were finally on your way, did you wonder what it was going to be like there, and what might be going to happen?

VM. Yes, of course, I made pictures for myself—which turned out to be entirely wrong—of Casals' house, and the lessons, and of me having a lesson, and of a congenial group of students laughing together in a café over a bottle of wine—all sorts of things. I knew I was on the threshold of a big adventure, and it was as exciting as it was frightening. It was just like any other threshold, and I had lots of imaginings about it.

JA. But you didn't particularly think then that the muddle might be dealt with?

VM. I didn't expect that Casals was going to tell me that I was in a muddle, no. Nobody ever had.

JA. Or that you even needed much help in any basic way?

VM. Well, I can tell you this: I said to myself—can you imagine?—'I mustn't let him get at my Bach!'

JA. Oh really? So you arrived in Prades.

VM. Yes, I arrived and went along to present myself, and he was very nice and kind and sent me off for a few days' rest. I'd already found a big room to stay in, with a stone floor and a door opening straight on to the main road—unbelievably noisy. There was a part for the kitchen sliced off behind glass, with a shallow sink and a pair of gas burners. There was a lot to get used to because I'd never really looked after myself before, all on my own, let alone in a foreign country.

JA. Did you do a lot of preparation for that first lesson?

VM. Yes, of course, I practised like mad. Then one morning Casals' very elegant niece came along to say my lesson would be at five-thirty that afternoon. So I went along, and I played him a page or so of the Schumann concerto. I was very nervous, and I said, 'I might not be able to manage from memory,' even though I had just won the cello prize at College with the Schumann. 'We do not use the music in Prades,' he said. I started off, and I wasn't giving a good account of myself at all, and then Casals stopped me and said, 'Just play naturally.' I said, 'I am,' but he shook his head and tried to find another word. But he couldn't, so he said, 'I mean *naturally*.' I thought, 'My God, does he mean that at twenty-one I've lost the ability to play naturally?' The thought was just too awful to contemplate, and I buried it, fast. So after I finished playing, he thanked me nicely, and then he said, 'You do not know what you are doing.'

JA. Just like that?

VM. Just pretty much like that. Very kindly, and perhaps even with a sorrowful shake of the head. Then he said, 'I can't even tell if you have any talent.' And that certainly came as a bit of a shock because no one had ever said that to me before! Then he said, 'If you are to have lessons, we must go back to the beginning. I expect you came here to perfect your Schumann concerto . . .' 'No, no,' I said, 'I want to find out about playing the cello.' And that was not so much because I loved the cello as because I felt I'd got into a deep hole, and I wanted to get out of it. So when he said 'You do not know what you're doing,' I felt I'd never heard more welcome words in my life. The relief was enormous. I knew we were going to get down to business, and I had absolutely no doubt at all from that moment that I was going to stay.

JA. What an extraordinary moment!

VM. He warned me that playing the cello was 'no joke' and that he could promise me only the beginnings of a basic technique by the end of the year, but he did undertake to teach me. So he asked me to come the next week with the Haydn Concerto in D, and I tried to protest because I had played it with the college orchestra at a concert only a few months earlier. But we thought and discussed, and we couldn't think of anything more suitable. 'No, the Haydn concerto,' he said. (Of course, at that time you realise the concerto in C hadn't yet been discovered.) Then I had to explain that my lessons would have to be at three-week intervals because my scholarship would only pay for ten lessons, and it seemed best to spread them out because I was determined to stay on for the Festival in the summer—besides which the scholarship foundation stipulated that I might not earn any money during the year. Neither of us felt it to be a very satisfactory arrangement, but it seemed the best possible in the circumstances. I don't have any written record of this first encounter, but the memory of it is as clear as yesterday.

JA. It's no wonder!

VM. So the first proper lesson, on the Haydn, happened the next week. We began with a scale, played very slowly, and he asked me why I kept my left-hand fingers so consistently at right-angles to the string (as I had always been taught), and he showed me that a willingness to turn my forearm just a little so that my fingers pointed more towards the bridge would give me much more freedom to stretch my hand. That was a revelation, and opened the door to a whole new conception of how things work. 'With elastic,' he said. 'You see, it's elastic.'

Then he soon spotted that my little finger had a tendency to collapse at the top knuckle. 'That is not good,' he said.' But I said, 'That's how it is.' 'But it is not good,' he said again. So I painstakingly explained that that finger had always *been* like that. And he said again, 'It is not good.' And then he showed me an exercise to practise. What I had to do was to put the first three fingers down on the string, and use this newly-discovered elasticity to lift the fourth finger right up in the air and then suddenly let it go, so that it hit the string with a loud 'ping.' It felt just like a frog's tongue, whipping out on a long stalk to catch a fly. And do you know, by the next lesson the weakness had vanished?

JA. That's incredible! Then did you go on to the piece?

VM. Yes. Then we began to work on the concerto, and he stopped me at the first note and said it was too sharp. So I adjusted it, and he said it was still too sharp. He kept on saying, 'It's too sharp' or 'too flat' until we found the one that made him say, '*That* one—but it is *piano*.' So I played it softer. 'But it is "piano" for a concerto.' Then it was too sharp again, and at last just right—'but with diminuendo,' he said. And so on, and so on. Then, we had to add the next note, another F sharp, but in the same bow. The shaping of those two notes together took another lot of time, and all the time something would go ever so little flat or ever so little sharp, and we had to maintain this same close attention until every contour, every aspect of those two F sharps was according to requirements. And whenever he said, 'That's it!' I was surprised, because I couldn't tell. I had thought every offering I made was good enough—and it just wasn't. So I had a 'blind ear,' you might say—he was leading my blind ear, my groping ear, and showing it where to go. So, at this lesson we only got through two bars of the concerto, but when I played them through, it was so beautiful it took my breath away.

JA. I can imagine!

VM. After that he showed me some scales to practise with a new fingering, and a few exercises. There were always very few exercises because, you see, it was the standard that was so exacting. There wasn't much 'material,' because with this sort of work a little material goes a long way.

JA. Yes, of course.

VM. So I went off for three weeks on my own after the lesson, and I found I could manage to keep myself working constructively, as I believed, for two of them, but by the third week I longed for reassurance and some guidance.

JA. Yes, I'll bet.

VM. So, at each lesson we worked in exactly the same way. We never went back to the beginning, and once we had got each phrase exactly right, I don't recall that we ever played it again—it seems that we always started a lesson where we had left off last time, but I think we must have gone back and played through what we did at the last lesson, and because it was still in good order we went straight on to the new bit and set to work on that. Once a phrase had been done to Casals' satisfaction, he would say, 'And then?' and we moved on to the next bit. So, all in all, in the first three months we got through the first three lines of the Haydn concerto in D.

JA. Gosh!

VM. But even though I'd been put through the refining of the intonation of every single one of those notes until he said 'That's it!,' *still* I didn't know—didn't *know*—which one was going to meet his requirements . . . and what with the modeling with the bow . . . and . . . everything else.

JA. Would he play with you at all, or for you, at that time?

VM. Yes, he played with me and for me all the time. If he didn't like what I did, he would play it himself so that I could hear and see and do my best to reproduce it. You see, in the course of the first three lines of the Haydn, you meet a bit of everything—upward shifts and downward shifts, the stretched positions and the angle of the hand and how to make the jumps and the percussion. And he was very insistent on the percussion, so that every note was articulated by the left hand fingers—frog's tongue style—so that you could hear every note even without the bow. Then when you added the bow, each note had a new distinctness—which was a revelation. I had no idea such clarity was possible.

JA. It must have been astounding!

VM. Yes! So I found all this work totally absorbing, though it was very hard. And I never had any inclination to go on to the next bit to see how it would go, although sometimes, in the early stages, I thought it might be nice to play through some simple little piece after my practice was done, to console myself, but when I tried, it sounded so awful it was unbearable. I soon gave that up. So I must have been beginning to hear better—and yet I didn't feel at all discouraged or unhappy.

JA. For a lot of people that could have been really disturbing or depressing.

VM. Yes, I think I'd have expected it to be too, but in fact, I remember thinking after about three months, at Christmas time, how I had left my family and my home and my country and all my friends. I wasn't even speaking my own language, and everything was new and foreign, and I was almost entirely on my own. I did have a kind landlady who would come and talk to me for fifteen minutes most evenings—though I knew this was partly to keep an eye on me. And I was very conscious of being watched as I went about my business in the town, and when I went into the corner shop, all the other customers would stop talking and turn to look at me. I didn't know how to ask for things, and I was very particular about not making mistakes, so I felt very conspicuous; it was quite an ordeal to go along and do my shopping, but it just had to be done. And when you add to all that the fact that Casals had with a single sweep of his hand taken my *profession* from me, it was all very devastating. I remember feeling like a chicken, plucked, gutted and hung up by the feet in a butcher's shop window—stripped of just about everything. And when I considered all this, I thought I ought to be entirely miserable. And then I thought, 'Actually, I'm *happy. I* know what it is; I'm getting the kind of nourishment I need, and I don't think I've ever had that.' And that was enough, you know, to make me contented—even though Casals had never said, 'Good,' or anything other than, 'Yes, and then?' There was no word of praise, nothing beyond the necessary—because he never did anything beyond the necessary.

JA. But you knew you were finally getting the essential ingredients.

VM. Absolutely. And after Christmas, when we moved on to line four of the Haydn, I realised that I had been changed, completely changed.

III

AFTER CHRISTMAS *(DECEMBER 1952)*

JA. So you came back from Christmas vacation.

VM. Where do you think I went for Christmas?

JA. 'Home for the holidays?'

VM. We didn't go 'home for the holidays!' I had a Christmas dinner of salami and cabbage with a little Christmas pudding my mother had sent me. Very good, too. And after that I went for a walk up to the place behind the cemetery, which was a favourite haunt of mine, for the view and for the hundreds of lizards basking and dashing about on the wall in the sunshine. And there were some clouds, the first clouds since

18

October—or at least the first clouds of this kind—that threw moving shadows across the hills. Like Scotland. So that first Christmas was quite an exquisite day.

So, right after Christmas we moved on to line four of the Haydn, and I discovered I'd been changed, in my ear and my hand and my brain, so that I felt like a different animal as we went on working in the same way.

JA. That same meticulous way?

VM. In the same way, on lines four, five, and six—but if you're working in this way, as it were, under a microscope, it's full of interest because you see all the beauties and everything that's there even in the most apparently ordinary little scrap or morsel of music. And in these next three lines there's a whole lot of new adventure to get to grips with.

JA. And all of that careful scrutiny reveals more and more of the whole musical import?

VM. Yes! It's all there.

JA. It's not just dwelling on technical details.

VM. Oh, dear me, no! It's contour and colour and . . . all sorts of . . .

JA. Everything that brings out the fullest meaning and expression in the piece.

VM. Everything there is.

JA. Yes!

VM. Yes. I don't remember whether this happened so early on, but sometimes we would play some fragment—say, three notes—taking plenty of time to see that all the contours were perfectly shaped and the colour perfectly graded as well as the crescendos and diminuendos—of which there would always be one or the other, if not one of each, in every note—because all notes either come or go. And this coming and going, to my mind, is something very special about Casals' playing; it has an extra dimension because the music not only travels along, it also recedes and comes towards you, which gives rise to something which I like to describe to myself as 'pace,' as distinct from tempo.

JA. Yes.

VM. So that you can go along strictly in tempo and yet you can hold the music still—for a moment—or you can let it come rushing at you at a great rate and still be strictly in time. As I say, I don't know whether we ever did that holding a tiny fragment up to the light to admire it and revel in its beauty in the first few weeks, but I had no sense—and I'm sure this was so—that he made any concessions to my being in the early stages. We dove straight in the deep end, because otherwise you set yourself a limited framework, and that's no way to begin if you're going to work in a big framework in the end. If you're going to work on a very fine level of meticulousness, you do so from the start. So this was what we straight away plunged into.

JA. Then you started to come for lessons more often, didn't you?

VM. Oh, yes. After four lessons, just before Christmas, Casals said to me, 'You must come every week.' Three weeks between lessons was obviously too long; the first two weeks were manageable, but the last was pretty demoralising. So I had to explain again about the terms of my scholarship, and that if I came every week, the money would have run out by February. Apart from the scholarship I had only just enough to live on. Then he said an amazing thing—he said, 'I give you five lessons.' I thought, 'Is he really going to give me five of these tremendously expensive lessons as a *present*?' I needed to be sure, so I stammered something or other, to which he said, 'Christmas present!' Well, of course I was overwhelmed and said so. Then he said, 'You need them'—which was abundantly true. And so we started on the weekly lessons.

JA. When you worked in this meticulous way, was that the same as playing something in 'slow motion,' as it were, so that you could sort of look at it through a 'magnifying glass,' as we were saying before?

VM. Oh, yes, yes, so that you could see all the colours and shades, and all the texture, where it tightens, where it loosens and where the turning moments are—so you wanted to take time to examine it and to bring it all into being—and you said that you think that other people don't do this?

JA. Yes. I don't think that most musicians *allow* themselves the liberty to do that—even if they understand how.

VM. I think they might not feel they can take the time to, because mostly we seem to be working against the clock in our professional lives to be ready for the concert in time.

JA. Yes.

VM. That makes me think of the Schumann that I played at my 'audition' lesson with Casals, because very shortly before I left college, a cellist friend in London, who was anxious to help me, thought he could do better than our teacher by telling me, 'Ah! But you must go to the *top* of the phrase.' He didn't say *how*, and I thought I was doing that anyway; so it wasn't very helpful.

JA. No.

VM. But Casals showed you *exactly* how to go to the top of the phrase. We looked at every footprint on the way to the top of the phrase. Gone was the launching out and hoping for the best that seemed to be all I could do in the past. In fact, everything with Casals was very much constructed—constructed and tailor-made to fit together. His craftsmanship was beautiful and yours had to be too—so that when you put everything together, it fitted, and the results were magical.

JA. 'Craftsmanship' is a wonderful word for it. But isn't the important thing to emphasize that there was no 'technique?' You didn't study technique separately from studying the music. You didn't get all your 'rudiments' learned and then somehow 'apply those to the music.'

VM. No, no. Apart from some scales and arpeggios and a very few basic exercises which got the music into your hands and limbered up your *attention* as much as anything else, you didn't get together a wardrobe or arsenal of techniques, bowings, or styles to bring out and put on as necessary. The music itself showed you what you needed to be able to do, and you worked at that, there and then, until you could do it.

JA. Here it might be worth pointing out to non-musician readers that acquiring technical skills first is the way that nearly 99% of classical musicians have been taught. They believe that there is no other way than learning technique separately and then continuing to work at maintaining it once they've acquired it. You may even go to a certain teacher to work on 'technique,' and then another to work on 'interpretation.' Or one teacher may switch back and forth: 'Well, we'll work this six months on technique—and then we'll . . .'

VM. Yes. 'We'll concentrate on your *bow* now,' or 'We'll concentrate on your left hand.' Of course, I was brought up with a good deal of that. I think that's a fine way to arrive at 'muddles,' probably because when you remove one part of what you're building, and you change and develop it and try to drop it back into the structure of the whole, it may not fit any more. Here we were in Prades, advancing very, very, very slowly on the widest possible front. I had to grapple with everything all at the same time, and that's why my brain was changed. It was as if in the first three months Casals had got inside my brain with his two hands and expanded it by stretching them apart.

JA. Did it occur to you then, at all, that the muddle might not be just 'your' muddle, but one that many other musicians might be in too, because most of them are taught in that same split-up way? That the muddle you were in was not necessarily unique to you?

VM. No, I don't think that crossed my mind. I think when people are in a muddle of any sort, they don't want anyone else to know—you're alone in your muddle.

JA. You didn't think then in terms of any generalisations or broader implications for others of what you were doing?

VM. Not then, no. But I did hope that when later I came to teach, as I wanted to do, that I would have the wherewithal to do it with much greater clarity than I had ever thought possible; but I also realised it would be very difficult, and a lifetime's work. Here I knew I was receiving optimally clear teaching, absolutely logical and defensible, like nothing I'd ever had—and, paradoxically, one of Casals' great strengths was that he used so few words!

JA. But it didn't occur to you to think of his way of teaching in any sort of world-perspective at all? I suppose you wouldn't have known much of what was being taught elsewhere, like in America, for instance?

VM. Oh, no, not at all. I didn't care, either!

JA. You wouldn't have been aware of general cello pedagogy as a 'field of study' in those days?

VM. No, not at all. I think when you're in a muddle, and your high priority is to get out of the muddle, then you're really not interested in other people and what's going on elsewhere.

JA. You hadn't been to string teachers' conferences and heard lectures on what'd been going on with European string teaching, for instance?

VM. Goodness, no! ESTA [European String Teachers' Association] and ASTA [American String Teachers' Association] didn't exist in those days, and there weren't even many master classes about either. Very different from now.

JA. Yes.

VM. So you see when Casals said, 'But *with life* and *with energy*, hmm?' you know, and '*elastic*!'—I felt that I was learning things I should have heard before, and then it made great sense. I thought, 'Why do people not think of those things?' I think he must have said, or made it very clear to me by his demonstrations, that, of *course*, we consist of elastic materials—we *are* elastic. I think he may have actually said this very early on, because I remember also he was showing me how, if I turn my left hand a little (a little more pronation—turning the wrist and palm towards the end-pin of the cello—sometimes considered old-fashioned), the ability to stretch between the first and third fingers and the second and third fingers is vastly greater. He pointed out to me that the third finger is a finger that finds it difficult to stretch. And I had even been through a couple of pages of brutal exercises in college to develop this stretch in the impossible 'square' position; in fact, one of the professors said, enthusiastically, 'My dear, do this one for three months and you won't *know* your hand.' And I thought, 'That's right. It'll be broken at the end of three months!'

Anyway, Casals stressed this elastic quality and showed me that this little bit of turning allowed the thumb to go farther down the neck of the cello, and then that the third finger would find it very much easier to stretch, and that the fourth finger, which has the tendency to get too sharp, goes down very close to the third finger much more easily— because it cannot stretch in that position. The fourth finger *can't* go too far. So this was a new idea altogether. In fact, I remember that from the very beginning of my cello experience, when I was six years old, this position with the palm turned toward the end-pin was considered rather old-fashioned and 'Frenchified,' and the up to date thing was to have the fingers at right angles to the strings—so that the fingers then could be trained to act like little hammers.

JA. And then you were supposed to move that right angle configuration up and down the strings, keeping it the same everywhere—except in the thumb position?

VM. Up and down, yes, from the first position to the second position, and so on. So the impression that I got from Casals was of a very 'ad hoc' sort of approach, moving from one note to the next as seemed best in the context, involving a lot of stretch—rather than the prevailing approach which seemed to say, 'We have these possibilities, this limited number of possibilities, and we deploy them thus—because it is traditional to do so.' I think that already, in the first three lines of the Haydn, Casals had given me fingerings that I found quite hard to believe—and, certainly, those fingerings demanded a great deal more boldness in jumping and reaching than I had ever encountered before. Certainly, the whole concerto which, after all, I had recently played, felt completely different under my 'new' hand.

JA. I suppose the experience was all the more poignant because it was with a piece that you had so recently worked on and performed.

VM. It really was. Yes, all the more amazing, the more amazing, yes. So it was, in the long run, a very good thing. It turned out, surprisingly, to be a really good thing to go back to something that I had very recently studied and do it all over again so soon.

Another of the things I learned in the Haydn when we got to the grupetto in the first phrase of the second subject was that *all* decorations, like this grupetto, start with an accent. He told me that a little note, among longer ones, must always have an accent. And the more it is a little note, the more it must have an accent. And to do that I found that I had, from an athletic point of view, to do something completely novel and vastly energetic—and it felt grossly wrong while I was doing it. It felt like using, you know, a sledge hammer to crack a nut. But what happened as a result of giving this terrific boost to the small note was that the note came out exquisitely clear, and the ornament was ravishingly beautiful. That was all.

JA. I remember Gillet[1] would also have me do something like that while I was studying with him. He would call it an 'instrumental accent,' when it wasn't actually marked as an accent in the printed music. And he would usually mark on my part, above the grace note or beginning of a grupetto, an accent in parentheses—almost as if it was only to be *thought of* as stronger, rather than deliberately played stronger, like a regular, printed accent. Do you think that was the same sort of thing at all?

---

[1] Fernand Gillet, first oboist of the Boston Symphony Orchestra (1925-1946) under Serge Koussevitzky, with whom Joe Armstrong studied from 1973 to 1975.

VM. Exactly the same thing! But for me on the cello it called for a real effort of doing, not just thinking.

JA. I'd certainly never had any other teacher or conductor speak in those terms, and most professional musicians I've described it to never seem to have heard anything about doing it either. But since Casals and Gillet were of the same generation, it seems to show something of the similarity in their understanding and approach that might have been lost. I think I also remember Casals saying somewhere that the grace note or grupetto is even an 'exaltation' of the note it's attached to—not just a frivolous trinket to be tossed on casually. It can have this tremendous, though subtle, emotional significance.

VM. Yes. I love the word 'exaltation!' When I offer this idea of an accent on the first note of an ornament to pupils, *whatever* instrument they play, or even if they're singers, it always seems to be surprising to them. But it always works!

Another important thing I began to discover was that not only the moment at which you launch a phrase, but also the moment at which you *re*launch—the moment at which you bowl it along a bit—is very critical. The moment at which you inject this fresh flow of energy is very often the least expected one. And this was a new kind of dynamic to me, a new process that was going on under the surface. It was not related to the bars as I had always thought. And, in spite of Casals having been unsure about my talent, I think I was innately musical; but I had, of course, been brought up on the idea that the upbeat is light and the downbeat is heavy. This was completely contradicted here in his way of relaunching the phrase. In the way we worked, many, many things were just upside down, turned upside down. To tremendous effect. And immediately, *immediately* it became clear why it was so.

JA. Yes!

VM. But where you have the phrase being shaped, as it were, at odds with the bars in which it falls, then you have a system of 'antagonistic pulls' which suspends your phrase so that it doesn't fall in among the bar lines. It doesn't get trapped. That's right. It doesn't get trapped in between the bar lines. It can fly. But you don't do this without *order* and *science.* You don't do this by simply 'letting it fly!'

JA. 'Liberty . . . but *with order*!' as Casals says in one of the recordings of his master classes.

VM. And again and again in my lessons!

But to go back to the question of 'pure technique,' we did do one exercise which actually took you through all possible configurations of the left hand, wringing from each string every possible combination of adjacent notes, until it was time to move on to the next string—and so on until you reached the A string, where you could go up and up as far as you liked. He said, 'This will take you one half of an hour.' I never found it took me half an hour. I found it took me almost all day . . .

JA. Ha, ha!

VM. . . . by the time I got it even to my own taste at home, because of course it had to be seamlessly smooth and immaculately in tune. So we did that, and I could see that it would actually put you basically through all the possible arrangements of the hand that there are in order to get the elastic going. So there was that, and there was the basic bowing exercise. So, in those respects, there was a sort of . . .

JA. 'Basic bowing' being the exercise where you try to get as many undulations per bow as you can?

VM. Well, not 'as many' as you can, because that's *endgaining*, and *competitive!*

JA. Oh, I see!

VM. But you learn to do many crescendos and diminuendos within one bow instead of ever practising lots of plain long notes. Because, as Casals was quick to say, quick to imply, there's really no such thing in music as a long, plain note. A note is always either going or coming; so there was no place for the long straight note—and yet that's what we're traditionally encouraged to practise—

JA. And we have 'long tones' that we practise on wind instruments.

VM. —because the ear doesn't cling to this uneventful plainness, so that in learning to do these multiple crescendos and diminuendos, you were learning to handle the bow in all the ways that you're going to want to among the myriad nuances of real music so that the ear goes on being intrigued. That's a very 'basic technique' exercise that has a very broad coverage. So it wouldn't be entirely true to say that he didn't have me work on technique *at all.*

And when I eventually finished studying with him, I thought, 'What I really need to do is perhaps an hour and half's practice a day of these basic things, plus some octaves, plus some scales in thirds and one or two special exercises.' And I believed then, as I still believe, that if I practised that way, then I should only have to *play* pieces. But, of course, when I returned to England, the demands of work quickly became too insistent, and I began to feel not safe. Well, I just didn't have faith enough to stick to this plan. And so I started practising the pieces, although I should have known better. So you see, I do believe in keeping 'technique' in trim!

JA. I know now that, for instance, if I don't have enough time to practise, somehow I've been able to convince myself that whatever happens in a performance will happen best if I can *at least* take time beforehand to do a chromatic scale in a series of long, separate pairs of half-steps in as true legato as I can possibly do each pair, meeting my own most stringent demands and specifications for getting from one note to the next. Also if I can do slow octaves in as true a legato as possible, and then play through the whole range of the flute chromatically by doing it in a series of two long tones on each pitch, articulating the first one pianissimo with a cre-scendo up to forte or fortissimo and then a fairly long diminuendo back to piano leading into a sudden sforzando attack on the second note—if I can do all that, then I've covered most of the essential things that I might have to do in any piece I'm going to perform, as well as I can cover them, maybe even *better* than I could do them by whittling away on or just playing through parts of the piece itself—particularly if it's one I know well and have worked on extensively. I'm also more ready to play all the pieces on a program than if I just touched upon the difficult parts of each—or even went all the way through each of them, for that matter.

VM. It's like stretching a canvas before you start a painting.

JA. Yes!

VM. I remember you also telling me once about the discipline that you were expected to impose on yourself at college by playing through loads of scales each day before you would start to work on a piece. So your discipline was to get through an awful lot, you see—and I said to you that the discipline with Casals was to *stop* the instant anything was not spot-on. Those are two opposite poles of discipline looking at each other, you know?

JA. The discipline with Casals was *not* to go on because it would only be perpetuating the habits you needed to change.

VM. Yes. Exactly!

IV

TAKING THE TIME IT TAKES

VM. Then when February came and I had to go and have my bow re-haired, I went round the mountain to Ceret with another student, Christopher Bunting, and his wife, and we had a very pleasant time with the luthier, Monsieur Ragot, who was a very charming man. We were trying his cellos, and of course he would have loved us all to buy them. So we were trying cellos, and Christopher was playing. He asked me if I would like to play the slow movement of the Haydn, and he offered to play an accompaniment for me. And I tried, but I found I couldn't do it. My 'new ear' just couldn't bear to hear so many imperfections. But it didn't worry me that I couldn't play it on that occasion, because I knew everything was eventually going to be all right. I could see it would take time, but I knew it would be all right. Time had a different value in Prades. You take the time it takes. I've heard that said somewhere else.

'JUST PLAY NATURALLY'

JA. Yes. It sounds like something we might say in the context of learning the Alexander Technique?

VM. Exactly. 'It takes the time it takes.' Very novel idea, that!

JA. Did you feel that it also might have had something to do with living in a remote mountain town and perhaps having people all around you who also take the time it takes for things? Did that contribute in any way, do you think, also to what Casals was giving you to do musically? There must have been many things that went together into one whole in the experience of both living there and studying with him in that setting.

VM. Yes. The pace of life was quite different. For one thing, I didn't have to attend any orchestral rehearsals or chamber music rehearsals, and I didn't have to get about London. I didn't have to practise the piano. I didn't have lectures to attend. I wasn't required to do any concerts. Nothing of that kind at all. The old life was full of urgencies. In Prades there was nothing that I had to do except practise the cello. But there were things like cooking my meals and washing my clothes that took an awful lot of time in those primitive conditions, and then there were other things of my choice, like spending a lot of time exploring the country. But as to living in Prades itself—well, there was not a lot of commerce going on, and although it wasn't tremendously in evidence, the people were cultivators. They'd have to wait. Have to wait for the harvest. There never were any apricots before July. You'd just have to wait for them. You dig the holes in autumn, then you plant the trees, and then you wait.

And so the way I was living my life was very much in tune with what was going on all around. But, of course, there were people who had to scurry. My landlady had to scurry down to the café every morning to peel the potatoes so there would be enough potatoes for everybody's lunch. Of course there were always things to be done. But most certainly that is one of the things that I value most about the whole experience—that it's so unusual to have this lack of obligation to do this, that and the other, to have so much time, to have no distractions, if you like, even from the other students. You see, I imagined, in my picture of what it was going to be like to be a student in Prades, a happy band of cellists all sitting late into the night over glasses of red wine in some café discussing fingerings, you know, and interesting philosophies and all the exciting things that students like to do. And there wasn't any of that, because for one thing, there were only five students, one for each day of the week. Casals liked to give only one lesson a day. And what's more, the five students were not particularly congenial to each other. In fact, there were some established enmities. One of the students had gone 'underground.' He slept all day and practised at night. We were all actually very, very busy practising.

JA. Who were the five students when you first got there?

VM. There was a Greek man, Eleftherios Papastavrou, who appeared briefly at college, and I knew him before, slightly.

JA. A cellist?

VM. A cellist, oh, yes. They were mostly cellists, of course. There was a Scotswoman fifteen or more years older than I, Vera Canning, who had studied with Casals before the war, as a young girl, and who was coming back after not having played for, oh, a dozen years or so while she was married, and who was having to get herself in shape again after her husband's death in order to be able to earn a living. So she was in a rather different state from myself because she'd already acquired plenty of skill—all from Casals too, which was just in need of revising—but having a time of it; so she was working in a different way from me. She was a good friend, but we didn't see a great deal of each other. We had very little time to spare in spite of there being so little else to do in Prades. There was also a Japanese man, Yoshio Sato, ten years older again, who was having a second year with Casals. He was a very delightful character. He didn't talk much. Very sweet. He was the one who practised all night and slept all day. His great treat was to have his hair permed. And there was a young German whom I never really saw, because I didn't even know he was there for a long, long time. He lived in a little school up in the mountains; as likewise did an American violinist, Alan Grishman. So those two I didn't even really know about. Of course, there was no occasion for us to meet at first.

JA. And were those five the five that were there all the time, or did they change after a while?

VM. No one was there the whole year, I think, except the Japanese man, the Scotswoman, and the violinist. I think the German cellist went back to Germany, and the Greek went off somewhere else towards the end of the year. And there were one or two additions—people who came for short visits. But on principle there was one lesson a day— 5:30—and it was either yours or somebody else's.

After some time, someone (I think it was the American violinist) had the idea of asking Casals if we could come and listen to his records, because he had a huge collection—mostly of himself and his friends. Casals liked the idea, and by about Christmas time, we began to go down there on Sunday evenings. And I remember that, after three months of not hearing any music except my own practice and my own cello lessons, when I heard it again, I realised how my ears had been cleaned. Not only had they had a rest from music, but I had also been having them sharpened. Polished up. Changed, by my work with him. So the music that I heard after three months was like music I had never heard before. Wonderful stuff!

JA. Were they mostly recordings of his playing?

VM. Yes. And we could choose. We would say, 'How about so and so?' There were also some orchestral and chamber music recordings from the first festival in Prades, which had happened the year before.

JA. Oh, I see. I didn't realize they'd already had a festival before you came.

VM. Yes. So there were already those recordings available plus some of his own old friends' performances. But we found that in a single evening we didn't want to listen to more than two or three works, and we wanted to listen to the same things again sometimes; so it took us quite a long time to get through the collection. Yet there wasn't a sense of limitation or lack of variety.

JA. Would Casals listen with you?

VM. Oh yes. There were two rooms, and he usually sat with his personal friends around a table, sometimes his niece and her mother and Catalan friends—friends who had come over from Spain in the same exodus as he. And quite a lot of them would turn up. There was one little lady who was known as 'La Scarole.' She used to go through the streets with a barrow-load of these lettuces to sell, calling out, 'La scarole, La scarole!' And she had a wide smile with more teeth in it than any one human being should possess. She was as wide as she was high, and one Sunday she arrived on Casals' doorstep, beaming, and said 'Bonjoor tout le mon*dah*!' in a very pungent local accent. And Casals put his fingers to his lips—because there was music going on—and patted the seat beside him, so she crept in and sat down, and beamed on everybody all evening. And the students, mostly, were in the other room or in the hall so as not to impinge. We didn't sit, necessarily. We stood, or we sat on the floor. We certainly didn't sit in rows. And a little talk happened between records. Very nice, very nice indeed. Sunday was: wash the clothes in the morning (it was hot water day), go for a walk in the afternoon, and go to Casals' house at six.

There's something else that I want to say about the first year which is not directly related to the work we did on the cello but which I found very surprising. It was one of the quite unexpected aspects of this whole experience. And that was, that while I had all day to practise in, in short bursts with rests in between, the practising took three and a half hours every day. I could not do more. Casals was beginning to give me so much to do, like all the scales and arpeggios in four octaves and so on, that I asked him, rather with my heart in my mouth, 'How many hours' practice do you expect me to do?' Because I was really only doing three, three and a half, and I thought, 'Maybe he's expecting me to do eight or nine.' So he looked me up and down, and then he said, 'I think you're young, you're strong, and I think perhaps three to three and one half hours in a day?' And I found that a big surprise and a great relief.

And when I was practising I would sit with my back to the clock, so that I could look out of the window, and when my concentration seemed suddenly to come to an end, I would turn around and find that I had been working forty minutes—except in the early morning, when it took me a little longer to get going. I wasn't counting the time, but I found that I had rhythms that I didn't know about. So it was interesting to see that in spite of being young and strong and having been tremendously motivated and paying all that much for my lessons—and, indeed being *given* so many lessons as a present—three and a half hours in forty minute blasts was my limit. And I think that was because the quality of the work was very high. It really was. I could stretch myself to do a bit more, but then the next day I was good for nothing. So there seemed to be some sort of profound physiological basis for the forty minute, three and a half hour habit.

Another thing that I also found interesting was my own rhythms on a larger scale. I found that about every six weeks I went into an ebb, for a day or two. I just gradually became depleted, and I couldn't bring myself to get practising. There was never any problem about practising, normally. That's what I was there for. But these particular days would drag by, and they came about every six weeks, not with reference to any other influence that I could see, because there weren't external influences. There was just me and this steady pace of work. And at those times I would go out into the country, which was very close at hand. I would go out into my landlady's property, which was a little field with apricot trees, and on the way there, I found I would pick up handfuls of earth and just run them through my fingers. I thought, 'What am I doing? This is really rather a mad thing to do.' Then I thought, 'No, it's not. I'm getting in touch with the earth, getting in touch with the basis of things.' And lying on the ground, too. I found that lying on the ground was very nice, even in winter. 'This is not sunbathing; just lying on the ground.' And I thought, 'Well, fancy that!' Something seemed to come up through the ground that I needed. Something came into my hands through this nice sandy soil. I just enjoyed the feeling of it. It was soothing and invigorating at the same time.

JA. So we're still talking about your first year?

VM. Oh, yes. In due course I came to the end of my scholarship money. After having had my five 'Christmas present' lessons, Casals had said, 'We must go on once a week.' That was perfectly obvious, so we did. And when we came to, I suppose it must have been about February, my money was running out; so I told him the next lesson would be have to be my last, and he said, 'Oh, no, keep coming.' So I went on coming.

V

SUMMER 1953

VM. Then early that first summer, the players arrived for the festival, mostly from America, and the orchestral rehearsals began.

JA. They arrived about the first of June?

VM. Something like that. I think earlier, about mid May, the first of the players were beginning to arrive. That changed the place utterly.

JA. Yes, I'm sure! So then did you stay through the festival?

VM. I stayed through the festival, yes.

JA. Which would have happened in July?

VM. Yes.

JA. Did you have lessons then too?

VM. No, lessons stopped when their rehearsals began.

JA. I see. Well, at the end of that first year of lessons then, had you felt at all by that time that you sort of . . .

VM. I knew I knew what I was doing.

JA. You knew what you were doing.

VM. I knew what I was doing. And at a lesson in late February or so, Casals had said, 'You can do it.' That was a shot in the arm. I wasn't ready, of course, to go off on my own yet. I had realised almost from the beginning that another year was going to be necessary.

JA. Yes, yes.

VM. Though I felt that I knew what I was doing, very, very much more, I wasn't ready to be on my own by any means. We'd learned the Haydn concerto, and we'd learned one short Schumann piece, and that was the sum total of the year's work—plus the 'technique.'

Incidentally, there had been two things that I brought with me from London that I wasn't to forget to ask Casals to do something about—a special request from my fellow students: 'Do, for goodness' sake, get him to do something about your vibrato and those terrible faces you make!' And I thought at the time, 'I must remember to ask him lots and lots of questions.' But almost as soon as I got to Prades, I realised that my questions were so much nonsense and entirely inappropriate. They were in the wrong 'language' and on the wrong subjects and altogether wrong. I would be asking the wrong questions; so I didn't ask any. I was getting many *much* too good answers to be asking any questions. And in the matter of the faces that I made, predictably, Casals paid no attention to my face. He paid no attention to my playing position. He made no attempt to change the length of my end pin or the angle of my cello. He left it as it was, because basically it was all right, and I could get wherever I needed to get on the cello. He pointed out that this is all you need. But as the way I got my fingers down on the strings changed, I suddenly thought, 'I'm not making faces any more.' And I called this phenomenon, to myself at the time, 'proper direction of energy,' which is almost exactly what I would call it now. Not long ago the same thing happened when I was giving a cello lesson. I could see quite vividly that when this pupil got 'that finger' sorted out, the thing that was going on in her jaw didn't happen. As I asked for, and got, more and more of what I wanted in the finger, there was progressively less and less going on in the jaw. And I believe I need not have mentioned the jaw. I did—but I believe I need not have. But it was very remarkable, in me, with Casals, that as my fingers began to behave better, my whole being began to behave better. And Casals never said anything about 'posture.' I don't think he ever even said anything like, 'Sit up.' But it became clear that only when you 'sat up' could you actually reach everywhere you needed to reach. Of course, I had the example of him sitting in front of me all the time. So without anything being said, a very great deal 'went in' . . .

JA. Yes!

VM. . . . along with fingerings and bowings and all the other things that I was having to catch from him sitting opposite, as they flew by.

So there were in that first year some tremendous shifts in my understanding—big, like the movement of the continents, you know. Such huge shifts that it may have taken me years to realise that they'd occurred.

JA. That didn't start happening until much later?

VM. Yes. Years later I began to realise that not everybody had experienced these things too and they often didn't know what I was talking about.

JA. Yes.

VM. So these shifts had happened unnoticed at a very, very deep level.

JA. In lessons you were just going on taking in, taking in . . .

VM. I was doing what was asked. I was obeying instructions—and being changed very profoundly indeed. I realised fairly early on, 'This is big stuff, this.' But it was all mainly for 'here and now,' and then the next thing would come. One thing at a time.

JA. 'One thing at a time.'

VM. Like life itself, really, come to think of it: 'this is what happens; and the next thing is: that.'

JA. Yes.

VM. One of the few things Casals *did* put into words was, '*Do only what is necessary.*' And I thought, 'Well, that's a sensible idea!' Sometimes what was necessary was far, far *more* than I'd ever done before. It was necessary, and I had to do it. But mostly it was less than I'd done before.

JA. I can imagine!

VI

SECOND YEAR

JA. Then, in the second year, did you start to go through repertoire more rapidly?

VM. Well, Casals had sent me away to practise the Haydn sonata in C during the summer holidays, and my friend Vera Canning said, 'You know, you'll spend the whole of next year on that one. It's a brute.' And I thought, 'Well O.K. If that's how it's going to be, it's going to be.' I wasn't expecting to get through things more quickly. I wasn't expecting anything. In fact, I had become thoroughly a 'non-endgainer,' you know. By then I really had. I had learned to stick with the means. And once the end had popped its head up satisfactorily, the work was done. You didn't have to worry at it or even repeat it 'to make sure.' It was on the shelf, or in the drawer, or wherever you keep it until you want it again. So, as Alexander said too, attention to the means really is what brings about the end we want.

JA. Yes.

VM. I can't remember when that became clear with Casals, because it wasn't a sudden revelation. It must have been becoming gradually clear from the beginning. Casals made it very obvious that if you plan and set up what you're going to do with enough care and completeness, you find you get first time the result you had in mind. That had already happened, you remember, at the very first lesson on the Haydn concerto, when at last we played the whole two bars that we'd been working on all evening, and it took my breath away.

And I also had to learn to hear what I'd done and not what I *thought* I'd done. That was very hard. It's so easy to be mistaken as to how you've actually played because you're so wrapped up in your intention that that's what you hear. You know, you have to plan. And then execute. Then only after that can you tell whether it was good or not. If the planning has been good enough, the result must be good.

JA. We might mention here that musicians are often *told* to pre-hear in their imagination what they're about to play, and in being so preoccupied with this pre-hearing, they may fail to hear what they *have* played, as you say. This is certainly the case with me and with most of my musician Alexander pupils.

VM. Mine too—and it's still hard for me.

JA. But at least you had a way of working then, at the end of the first year?

VM. Yes, I did. So I worked away contentedly at my Haydn all summer in England in the new way, and when I came back in September, he said to me, 'You have the intonation. That's good, you have the intonation.' And that was unexpected and a really great pleasure to hear. It was positively thrilling, actually, to realise I *could* work on my own now.

JA. To have him finally suggest that you had accomplished something substantial?

VM. Yes, and he had said, 'Good.' Then he said, 'And then?,' asking for the second movement. I don't think I'd even looked at the second movement. And there and then in the lesson we went pretty quickly through it. I don't think we spent more than one lesson each on the second and third movements. Three lessons altogether. This was a very big advance in my speed of working! It was clear that I had begun to know what I was doing. Then he said, 'What would you like to do next? What shall we tackle next?' And I told him I'd never learned the Dvorak concerto. He said, 'Oh, it's very difficult. But—very well, we shall learn the Dvorak concerto.' So I brought it along, and it *was* difficult. I remember it seemed like having to scale a great wall of unknown height and unlimited width. It took six lessons to get it under my belt. It was a wonderful experience—hearing myself do all that. It's such a lovely 'grateful' work. It was very good to have done it at that stage, immediately after the two Haydn pieces. So on we went. Next, after Christmas, we started on the fifth Bach suite. I was astonished at the rate we were going. (I know Casals was astonished at the progress I was making too, because he had said so to a former pupil who came to visit him, and she told me. 'Un progrès incroyable,' he'd said to her. I was very pleased to hear that!)

That second year I learned a tremendous mixture of stuff. After the Bach came the *Five Pieces in Folk Style* by Schumann, which I'd never even heard. They became and still are a great favourite of mine. I learned them in the depths of a terrible winter, and I remember sitting over one of the pieces in the kitchen—having gone out in the morning, I suppose, to collect wood to make a quick flare-up in the stove. By now my landlady had decided to move me upstairs to her own apartment—since she was out all day—and I could practise in the tiny kitchen if I carefully moved the table out of the way so that I had just about room to bow on all four strings. I had bought a piece of cotton to make a curtain for the doorway so as to keep the heat in, and I heated a brick in the oven to put under my feet, and I had a magic chemical hot-pad, activated by a teaspoonful of cold water, which I tucked in my trouser-band, and I was wearing a coat, which made my arms very heavy—which didn't help, I realised—and a pair of cut-off gloves, and a scarf, and a woolly hat, and everything I could muster. It was as cold as that.

JA. Gosh!

VM. Yes! And I used to put a little bowl of water on the windowsill outside and amuse myself by watching how quickly the ice formed on it.

So I sat there working at the third of the Schumann pieces, and I thought, 'I've been here rather a long time.' I looked at my watch, and I found I'd been there five hours! I'd no idea it had been so long. That was the first and only time that my forty-minute attention span had failed. I think I was simply so cold that I'd got a touch of hypothermia and I really had got rather sluggish in the brain! The prevailing indoor temperature was two degrees above freezing that winter.

JA. How on earth did you keep warm enough?

VM. Well, I would go out into the country and collect wood to burn. Of course I got awfully warm while I was fetching wood. That was splendid. So was the fire, while it lasted! But I was cold in bed at night. I was cold in the morning. I was cold in the afternoon, and cold in the evening. We really were on survival tactics, and the students would invite each other, not to a meal or anything like that, but 'Do come on Thursday, I'll be lighting a fire'—or 'I've got a new gas bottle for my radiator. Come and have some of my heat.' And so we would go and huddle together. The cinema was open once or twice a week, and part of the attraction for everybody in town was that it was heated and they sold hot punch in the foyer. So it was also a good place to go, whatever film was showing. We all became much more friendly at that time than hitherto.

JA. So once the elements of playing were all there at your command and you started going through more repertoire, you and Casals were really able to work together as musicians during your second year?

VM. I realise it was beginning to feel like that, though at the time, I was too busy to notice. But he did say later on when I was overcome with the honour (and thrill) of having him play the piano with me, 'No, no, we are two musicians.' You see the Dvorak was exciting because I was moving on from the intricacy and delicacy of the Haydn pieces and having to expand—without losing the accuracy—into the great long lines and the grandeur of the Dvorak. And then the Bach . . .

VII

SECOND YEAR—
OTHER STUDENTS

JA. Who were the new students in the second year?

VM. It becomes a little difficult for me to remember who came when. The first year is quite clear because these were the people that I gradually came to know as I was getting to know the place, and getting used to the new kind of life. For instance, I don't remember when Marta Montañez, whom Casals later married, arrived. But I do remember that when she had just arrived, aged 18, I took her to the Post Office to send a cable to her mother in Puerto Rico. The clerk got out his directory and ran his finger up and down the list of countries. "Voilà! he suddenly exclaimed.

'Costa Rica!' Marta said, 'No. Puerto Rico.' So he ran his finger up and down the columns again, page after page, and found Costa Rica again. 'Voilà, je l'ai!' Marta insisted on Puerto Rico. So a third time he set off to find this elusive destination. And he finally slammed the book shut, as he said decisively, 'Puerto Rico n'existe pas.' How's that for a traumatic beginning to her Prades adventure?

JA. Amazing!

VM. I hadn't expected such a varied bunch of students. I didn't expect anyone from Japan, for instance. I'd imagined a group of Europeans. Curiously enough, there was only one French person in all the three years, and that was for a very short visit. Around Christmas of the second year, I remember quite a lot of people came—my teacher, Olive Woodington, for one. She came whenever she could arrange to have a few weeks away from her teaching. There was a Dutchman from the Concertgebouw Orchestra, and there were Bruno Schrecker and John Franca who had both been at college with me. And then, instead of the Japanese man, we had a Chinese girl, I-Lan Tsao. And she was an interesting girl. She came from Hong Kong, and her husband stayed at home, except that he came to see her at Easter. Then next Christmas she went home and had a baby, and left it with her mother, the baby's grandmother. This was the fourth time she'd done this, and I was quite shocked at so different an attitude to maternity from my own. And she said that when she completed her training she would teach in Hong Kong, and all of her pupils would live in their house and have a lesson *every day*. I don't know if that came to pass. Her husband was also a musician, and they felt that things were pretty shaky in that part of the world, and the best way they could possibly use their money was to educate themselves as fully as possible as their best investment for their future. So there was the Chinese girl, and I think she stayed for two years.

Then a cluster of people came for a very short time. There were two women who came from Edinburgh, one of them Australian. Funny, this proportion of Scots. Oh yes, and of course the other person who was there throughout the second year was John Franca from London. He'd also been at college with me. He used to come galloping along and tell me *all* about his lesson. I didn't terribly want to hear all about his lesson. Every lesson day, I came home and wrote it all down in my notebook. I didn't think of telling anybody about it, but I did write it all down. I don't know if John Franca came with the *intention* of staying two years, but he did. Bruno stayed a full year. And all the other people stayed less time. Then of course in the third year the Australian violinist, Ronald Woodcock, came. We learned the Brahms double concerto with Casals later on. And there was Bernard Vocadlo, a Czech from London who went to Australia—eventually. He wasn't very communicative but was very earnest and serious, and he seemed to practise a lot. In fact, I think everybody else probably practised more hours than I did. And there was Carlos Paniagua from Guatemala, who was a marvelous dancer. The social scene in the second and third years was much more lively!

JA. So most of the people who came while you were there really didn't stay as long as you did?

VM. No. Vera Canning came for one year. Then she felt that she needed a second, so she enrolled, as it were, in a second year of lessons. Then she had this terrible accident to her hand at the very beginning of the second year and had to go back to London.

JA. Did you have a sense then that any of the other students were really getting down to the basic stuff, as you were?

VM. I knew many weren't, because they were better than I was when they came.

JA. Oh.

VM. Nobody was in the state of muddle that I was. They *may* have been in a state of muddle, but I didn't think they were.

JA. Yet, on the other hand, if they were 'better,' I suppose they were 'better' enough that Casals probably wouldn't have done all these essential things with them, even if they had needed them, because he wouldn't have wanted to interfere too much with their 'professional accomplishment.' Don't you suppose, because of that, he would have dealt with things on a more superficial basis with them? Or would he have felt that they automatically understood the kinds of things that he went into with you in such great depth?

VM. I can't imagine that he didn't see everything there was to see, since he was the only person in the world who saw that I didn't know what I was doing. How did he not see exactly what was going on in the other people too? But when I've talked to some of them since those days, I've found they didn't seem to have picked up the same things as I did. It was as if they'd been to a different Casals.

JA. What about John Franca?

VM. John Franca did, but somewhat differently. He became a lovely player, though he never became at all well-known. Yet a special 'Casals quality' was always there. He said once that he was going to give a talk about Casals. And he did so. But he told me that if I were going to give a talk, mine would be a much more 'spiritual' talk than his.

He had sensed that I was having a different experience from him, although I don't remember talking about it very specifically. Anyway, being, as I am, so entirely practical, I was a bit taken by surprise when he said this, and I don't think that he meant, 'You'd be fancy about it,' you know, and sort of airy fairy—anything like that. But I think that he felt that my experience was a bit more, well . . .

JA. Deeper, perhaps?

VIII

DIFFERENT LADDERS

VM. . . . Well, you know how I recently said to this young Italian cellist, in my limited Italian, 'You'd assume that studying with Casals for three years would jump you several rungs up the ladder to being a successful soloist, wouldn't you? But, you see, it turned out that it was a different ladder.' It was the very limitations of my vocabulary that made me hit on this very good picture, and I saw clearly and suddenly as I said it how true it was. So I think John probably realised that I was on a different ladder—though I didn't myself.

JA. Even when I think of the various well-known musicians I've come across who knew Casals or claimed to have been his pupils and to have been inspired by him, it seems that they surely should have got some of that deeper stuff too. Yet, when I hear them play or talk about what they learned from him, it's always seemed to me to be on a much more general and superficial level than the kinds of things that you seem to have received.

Just the things that you've already delineated about what you actually went through with him in these early stages already sound infinitely deeper—getting much more to the very core of things about music and cello playing. But maybe there are different levels of teaching . . .

VM. Perhaps there are.

JA. . . . and if you've got a chance, as a teacher, to really help someone in a fundamental way, and if they're willing to go along with you and go more deeply into things, then you can work with them differently than you would with someone who just comes mainly to play for you and receive some comments, tips, or affirmation, with no intention of staying with you for very long. Or even if they do stay on, they might not really be interested in having you help them with these essential elements.

VM. I think that's a factor. It isn't what they want, and if they've come for a very short amount of time—five or six weeks—what can you do in that amount of time? I mean, if someone comes to *me* for lessons just for a short time, I can't help treating them a bit differently. And then possibly, as you just said, there might be different levels of teaching, and possibly different levels of learning too. It's obviously so, isn't it? It depends on what you're looking for, just as what fish you're trying to catch decides you on what bait to use. I dare say it's *because* Casals did this sitting opposite you and saying 'No, but you must do it like this,' and you did it like that, that his teaching got to so deep a level—with me at least. But when I tell people that Casals said to do it 'like this,' they of course raise their eyebrows, and say 'Who wants to copy someone else's playing?'

JA. Yes, I've had the impression that people think he *made* his students play his way . . .

VM. But he *did*!

JA. . . . and that you had no choice, and therefore were just a sort of carbon copy of him.

VM. Well, how many carbon copies of Casals are there? Yes, that's a very reasonable objection, I think; but when I was doing what he was doing, sitting opposite him—what I was doing was using the same amount of bow, the same amount of stretch, the same this, that, and the other. It was the 'carpentry' of the construction that I was learning. The result apart, it was the *means* that I was reproducing, and those means were darned good. *They* were what brought about the result. It wasn't just making it sound superficially 'like' what he did.

JA. Because you were working with so much more of the 'soil' of the music?

VM. Oh, yes.

JA. The 'earth' of the music.

VM. We were digging in the ground.

JA. He wasn't just saying, 'Oh, now, this movement must go this way, and the tempo should be such and such.' You weren't working so much with surface elements like that. You were working on the nitty-gritty . .

VM. . . . on the 'how.' I was digging in my own depths, never mind the music's!

JA. . . . at the 'means-whereby' of playing, to use a phrase from the Alexander Technique?

VM. Yes. Absolutely. Shining a searchlight on these things. Examining them all like an archaeological dig. 'What have we got here, what is this exactly?' I mean, it would have been absolutely absurd for him to say, 'Let me hear how you do it, my dear. Yes, I like that. Carry on.'—you see?

JA. Of course!

VM. That would have been absurd. And when I went back to England, after my first year, I was telling my story to one of the professors at college, and she said, 'But you must be *you*, my dear.' I thought, 'Well, I'm not formed yet in any way at all. I will not be able to *help* being me. Ever. For better or worse.' So I feel that the 'copying' of Casals was no danger at all. It would be a pity if, now, I listened to his recordings regularly and modeled my version on his.

But when I do very occasionally listen to his recordings, what I think is not, 'Oooh, I want to sound like that,' so that I copy the superficial effect. What I find, rather, is, 'My goodness, that bass note there is far more important than I thought, because it gives rise to the whole phrase'— or, 'Gosh this needs more time: it all falls into place given more time like this.' That sort of structural thing.

IX

INTERPRETATION

JA. Yes. So, such a thing as 'learning Casals' interpretation,' or dealing with 'interpretation' as most people think of it, wasn't really a thing you did with him.

VM. Well, I don't understand the word 'interpretation' in this context. We shouldn't 'interpret.'

JA. No.

VM. 'Interpretation' seems to imply change.

JA. Yes.

VM. Modification.

JA. Then you're intellectually deciding to impose your idea on what's there, rather than working in a way that you're . . .

VM. . . . letting it work on *you.*

JA. So if you're working with the nitty-gritty, the 'means-whereby' and the 'earth' of the music, then it works on you, and it's just revealed—more and more as you go along.

VM. I think so, yes. But not that easily.

JA. You don't put yourself as a person, an ego, above the music.

VM. Oh dear me, no.

JA. That's what the word 'interpretation' usually implies, why it has so little appeal.

VM. Yes.

JA. That 'I' with my 'superior knowledge, from all my years of study and research, etc.' can 'interpret' Bach or Schumann or whomever for these people who are 'my' audience.

VM. Oh, no no no.

JA. But it also certainly points to something deeper about your attitude, and presumably to Casals', towards music in general, that few performers have these days because they think so much in terms of 'my interpretation' and 'your interpretation.' Or on the other hand, you've got the performer who says he 'plays for God,' or 'God plays through him.'

VM. Yes, or, 'When I play Bach I feel like Jesus Christ,' as I heard one famous cellist say.

JA. Yes.

VM. That reminds me of two things. That extraordinary experience the first summer, when all the famous musicians came for the festival and Casals recorded the Schumann concerto for Columbia Records. The rest of us who were there listening were all hoofed out of the building when recording began, because it was more or less a ruin[1] and we might have

---

[1] St. Michel de Cuxa (900–1100, A.D.), a Romanesque abbey situated at the foot of Mount Canigou above Prades. Portions of the ruins of the abbey were taken to the Cloisters museum in New York, but the original site has been restored since the time of the Prades Festivals in the 1950's.

made a noise on the gravel floor. And I, knowing the building from my many walks thereabouts at the foot of Mt. Canigou, knew that if I hurried up round the hill at the back, I would find a window-ledge where I could sit. The building was partly carved out of the mountainside, so this window was at ground level outside, but far above the 'platform' area downstairs inside. So I sat in the aperture of this window which had no glass—just a window hole—and I was able to look down on Eugene Ormandy conducting the orchestra and Casals playing the Schumann, recording. Actually, it was far more comfortable to look out on the landscape, so that's what I did. But the playing was so remarkable, so extra specially remarkable, that I just had to look in. I looked down, and for a moment I couldn't see Casals. I could see the orchestra, I could see the conductor, I could see the cello—and there was nobody playing it! And I thought, 'But of *course* he isn't there. That's his job, to be absent so that Schumann can happen.' That was only for an instant, but it was an amazing instant. I'd been prepared for that insight by the kind of work we'd been doing. Because, you remember, I told you about the early stages and how we chipped away at the Haydn. We did this bit and then that bit, and when each bit was right, we put it away and went on to the next bit as though we were preserving fruit for next year—you know?

JA. Yes.

VM. Once it's sealed, you put it away! You don't disturb it. And then when I suddenly was called to go and play to my scholarship people in two weeks' time, on Easter Monday in Edinburgh, I burst into tears and went to ask Casals what I should do. He said, 'You play the Haydn.' I thought, 'I play the *Haydn*?' (Because I hadn't been practising it. I hadn't even looked at the first movement in two months!) And he said, 'You come on Friday.' I went on Friday, and we played the Haydn! We took all the preserves out and set them out in order, and lo and behold, there was the Haydn concerto! It was absolutely amazing. And that this nitty-gritty, earth-level, foundation-level, microscopic, filtering, testing work, searching work, should actually result in *music* without further tinkering or embellishment, I think was a sort of preparation for that moment of enlightenment, there, listening at the window to the Schumann. The music happens when you're not there. Your business is to get the muck out of the way. Clear the way. As I saw it, Casals was a conduit for the music, and he had to clear out the rubbish and encrustations to allow it to flow

through cleanly. And that's our job. I suppose it's our job as 'interpret-
ers,' if we must use that word. But out of my 'pipe' I hope not to produce, to push at you, an 'interpretation.' I'm kept too busy just keeping
the pipe clear, so that the music can flow.

X

ALEXANDER LESSONS BEGIN
& LINKS APPEAR–1968

JA. And of course then it's so obvious what the Alexander Technique has to offer us as performers in becoming better 'pipe cleaners.'

VM. I think it's indispensable.

JA. Yes.

VM. Yes, because with Alexander, you're learning to meet the flowing current of what has to be done in every moment of daily life without interfering. All those 'undesirable habits' that are clinging to the inside of the pipe. These things have to go.

JA. Do you think it's worth digressing here and saying something about when you first came in touch with the Alexander Technique and you suddenly saw that it had something to offer that reinforced what you learned with Casals?

VM. Oh yes. Yes, if you like. I was thoroughly happy with what I had got from Casals, not feeling there was anything missing at all—except in myself, in my own discipline, in my own searching. At the end of the three years I felt that I had been sent home with the tools. I was absolutely certain of that. Casals said so, for one thing! He said, 'There is nothing you cannot do,' and I knew that that was true. And I thought, 'Well, here I have my trowel and my saw and my hammer and my chisel and all, and the skill in dealing with these things will grow as I tackle everything that comes my way.' Of course by the time I was teaching to earn a living, and having to deliver a performance at perhaps five days' notice, for instance—well, you can't work in the ideal way then, unless you have colossal self-discipline, which I hadn't. I'd sort of run out of self-discipline through fatigue, perhaps. But all the same, a lot of very interesting things came up. I found I loved teaching. I'd always wanted to teach, and I became passionately interested in teaching the cello. By about 1968, my husband, who had a very bad back, was having Alexander lessons, and when he said, 'I'd like you to have lessons; I think you'd find it interesting.' I said immediately, 'I haven't time. And we can't afford that.' So far as I was concerned, that was a genuine and watertight reason. It was the truth. But then one day I went to pick him up from a lesson, and I met his teacher, Jeanne Day. And as soon as I saw her I thought, 'Aha! Yes, I want what she has, whatever it is.'—and my objections somehow miraculously dissolved. I realised that my objection had really been that this 'Alexander Technique' sounded a bit strange, but I could see *she* wasn't strange.

So I went along to my first lesson, and Jeanne began to teach me in language that I recognised. This was nearly fourteen years after I'd gone to Casals, and I thought, 'I've heard this sort of thing before, and I heard it from Casals.' So there was an immediate and exciting resonance between these two things—that which was coming in, and that which was already there. Even very early on, say after two lessons, I thought, 'I've got to have a whole lot more of this if my cello teaching is going to develop.' I'd thought my cello teaching was developing splendidly, but I realised there was a whole lot of new information here that I must have. I felt you can't really set about teaching any instrumental skill without this knowledge from Alexander. Something's missing otherwise, and that's not good enough.

ALEXANDER LESSONS BEGIN & LINKS APPEAR – 1968

JA. Yes. I remember thinking *exactly* the same thing about teaching flute.

Has it ever occurred to you, maybe in retrospect after having so much Alexander experience, that either your manner[1] or your conditions[2] of 'use' of yourself might have been a factor in your receiving more from Casals than some of the other people who came to him who might have had poorer use than you?

VM. I've never thought about that in quite those terms. But as you say it, I remember that I have an old photo of myself at sixteen, slumped and crunched over the cello. And I know how I felt. I know I felt terrible because the muddle was at quite a peak in those days. And it was at an even greater peak when I left college, but I had enough nice certificates and prizes and accolades of this sort and that sort to set against my sense of muddle. But at that young age I think the tendency to 'good use'—which after all is normal in a healthy young animal—may be pushing at the crust of the mis-use and sometimes breaking through, as I saw in my own twenty-ish sons. So just possibly it's true that my 'use' wasn't so terrible, but I can't imagine that I was using myself well with a muddle like that going on inside. But I had a degree of confidence given to me by those 'accomplishments,' so that I was perhaps 'held up' by them in some way. And when that false bolstering was brushed aside, Casals had a very amorphous mass to work on. And he worked on that, as you might say, from the periphery right to the core. He worked on it through my eyes, by making me watch him. And simply watching him, opposite me, you see—it's very hard to watch someone who's 'going up' and not to 'go up' too. Or not catch some of it. And then he appealed to my fingertips with all their 'potential'—just bursting to be liberated. And working with my fingers in the way that we did developed their sensitivity. I think it was just my readiness to learn, perhaps, that contributed the most to giving me the kind of energy that would have made me 'go up' in Alexander terms.[3] I did know that while he was working with me he wasn't just working on my cello playing. And after the Alexander lessons began, I

---

[1] The degree of muscular, ligamental, and tendinous shortness, length, or flaccidity that exists in us no matter how freely or tensely we react and carry ourselves.

[2] Our way of reacting to stimuli and our general carriage of ourselves in daily life, which we are able to have conscious control over from moment to moment.

[3] In the teaching of the Alexander Technique, the general, overall experience of lengthening in stature that is brought about when the postural mechanisms are working in an integrated way is sometimes called 'going up'—as opposed to 'pulling down' or 'collapsing,' which is what we often do when we're striving too hard to accomplish a task, overreacting to a situation, or when we're lethargic or very fatigued.

realised he'd also been working on my 'use of myself.' And of course Casals was also pouring very good stuff into my ears, and he was really *making* me listen. And as I found one day, years later, teaching a group of small boys playing chamber music, when I got them looking and listening (and seeing and hearing!) I inadvertently got them sitting up. Because you can't be perceiving acutely well without 'going up.'

JA. You can't be attentive, alert, and awake . . .

VM. That's right . . . without 'going up.' So not only was Casals appealing to my eyes, ears, and fingers to be constantly engaged, but he was also making me really, really use them. And that must lead via the super-sensitive periphery right to the core. I had to really, really use my eyes because, remember, in my first lesson he said, 'We don't use the music in Prades.' So I never took the copy along. And so when he gave me fingering—because, as I said, he was sitting opposite me—I had to reverse this visual image and translate it to 'over here.' And then having translated all that to my side of 'the mirror,' I had to *remember* it. It didn't get written down until I got home after the lesson—and that was a huge expansion of my brain, a huge expansion of my visual attention. At the same time he was really making me listen, because he was telling me, 'That F# is not in tune. It's still flat,' and 'Now it's sharp again,' and I had not the faintest idea of the distinction. So he was just getting into my ear and stretching it, stretching it, stretching it until at last I was able to pick up these nuances. And he was doing exactly the same thing with how I used my fingers. And when there's that much stretch going on in the ultra-sensitive extremities—eyes and ears count as extremities—you're going to get something exciting happening right to the core.

JA. And it *has* to take you up!

VM. With such a tremendous demand at the places where it counts, where there's such a concentration of nerve endings, it couldn't be otherwise.

JA. Yes! So just in the wonderful example of Casals' use of himself while you were sitting opposite him he instilled or inspired in you an improved manner of use of yourself as a whole too; but there could conceivably be other people who, because of their poor conditions of use or attitude, etc., wouldn't particularly have picked up on any of that or received any of that from sitting opposite him.

VM. Oh, I suppose it's possible that some people might be impervious to it. But not everyone got 'the extremities treatment' the way that I did!

JA. I suppose not. But from your experience over the more recent years as an Alexander teacher, of being more able to assess people's conditions and manner of use, you know there can be a vast difference from one person to another . . .

VM. Yes.

JA. . . . and the less free, attentive, open, and 'up' someone is, it really stands in the way of their receiving the kind of total influence that you were getting?

VM. Yes. And it was going to stand in mine, wasn't it, when I heard Casals' Bach recording before I heard him in the flesh, and I thought, 'I'm not going to let him get at my Bach!'?

JA. Yes!

VM. If I'd gone on feeling, 'I prefer the Schumann *my* way' or 'I like my interpretation of the Elgar,' that would have made an impervious membrane between him and me, as regards this transmission of 'use.' Very much so. Oh, it was because I was desperate that I got so much! *That's* when you drop the seed in hungry ground, isn't it, and it can grow?

JA. Yes! So was it mainly the actual *experience* from your early Alexander lessons that was bringing you more into the same state that you would be in when you sat opposite Casals and you would play well; or was it mostly the concepts of the Alexander work that seemed the same as Casals', or both together?

VM. It wasn't the concepts at all. It was the general flavour of paradox in the Alexander teaching, I think. 'Don't *try*,' 'Let it happen; stop interfering; wait for it and the right thing will happen by itself if you keep out of the way.' Casals said or implied all of those things. But above all it was that both teachers were telling me all the time *not to do the wrong thing.* Casals said, 'No,' and Jeanne said, "Stop.' She was bringing into everyday life the rigourous attention to preventing the wrong thing from happening, as Casals had been specifically in my cello work. Clearing out rubbish. I felt I'd come home!

XI
ALEXANDER'S DISCOVERY

JA. Do you think we should describe the Alexander Technique in detail here for readers who might be unfamiliar with it?

VM. Yes, good idea.

JA. Shall we start with some background on Alexander as we did with Casals?

VM. Yes. Because their early stories had some similarities, in that they both came up against problems with the conventional teaching in their respective fields that they solved in groundbreaking ways.

JA. Why don't you start, and I'll just chime in.

VM. Well, Alexander was a close contemporary of Casals. He was born in Tasmania in 1869, and even though he lived a rather countrified kind of existence, he got the idea that he really wanted, above all things, to be a Shakespearean actor. So he set his mind to this, took some lessons in voice production, and he was being pretty successful towards the end of the nineteenth century in Sydney and Melbourne as a reciter of excerpts from Shakespeare and comic and dramatic monologues.

But then he noticed that he was developing a worsening tendency to get hoarse by the end of his recitations, to the point of even losing his voice. Of course, if you're going to get hoarse and even lose your voice, you aren't going to have a future as an actor. He went to doctors and voice trainers in search of a solution, but none of the treatments they pre-scribed was in any way useful. Even the resting of the voice—that is so commonly seen as a solution to overuse problems—did no lasting good. Then Alexander said to his doctor, 'Could it be something I'm doing with my voice as I recite?' The doctor agreed that it must be, but he couldn't tell Alexander what it was. So Alexander decided that he must try to find our for himself what he was doing wrong. Then he got himself some mirrors, and he watched himself doing what he usually did.

JA. Reciting lines, from Shakespeare.

VM. Yes. At first it looked perfectly normal, but then he began to notice that there was a certain thing that he consistently did with his head in relation to his neck, especially as he came to the climax of his speeches —which anyone will do if you ask them to shout at you. They'll stiffen their necks and thrust their faces towards you. Which, as he saw it in his mirrors, could also be described as pulling the head back and down. Then he thought, 'What would happen if I stopped doing that?' So he gave himself the instruction to stop doing that—and saw that he did it anyway, as if he'd never given himself any such instruction. Then he thought, 'Aha! If you are pulling your head back and down,' which is what he saw, 'what you have to do to correct that, is to put your head forward and up.' It's obvious. (This is a very common and unhelpful practice in teaching various skills—to recommend doing a lot of the 'op-posite' of the wrong thing so as to put matters right.)

Then he went back to the beginning of his passage, and he gave himself the instruction to put his head forward and up, *which he felt he was doing*—but as he watched in the mirror, he saw that he wasn't. So he'd made two rather appalling discoveries. The first was that he didn't know what his own head was doing—he'd assumed he was in charge of his own head. And the second was that he couldn't even trust his feelings about what was going on in himself. But he persisted, and found what he had to keep doing was *stop* himself just before he spoke. It took him a very great deal of time to find the crux of the problem, because, as he realised, he was going to have to reorganise what was happening between the moment of getting the idea of speaking and actually speaking.

JA. The 'critical moment.'

VM. The 'critical moment.' Not a moment that any of us are much aware of the existence of.

JA. Because we're thinking so much of what we're going to say, that . . .

VM. . . . we're not thinking of *how* we're doing it. We assume that everything's going to be all right.

JA. In other words, we're 'endgaining,' in his terminology.

VM. Absolutely. Gaining our ends without attention to the 'means-whereby,' in his terminology. And you could say that Alexander had got into quite a muddle of his own at that point.

Now, he found eventually that in order to get round the problem of his head pulling back he needed to maintain what he called a 'lengthening of stature.' And you notice, in his book *The Use of the Self*,[1] that he says 'maintain a lengthening,' He doesn't just say, 'stand tall.' This process of lengthening had to continue *while* he was doing the thing that had been making him shorten.

JA. He doesn't say, 'I had to adhere to a certain posture.'

VM. Absolutely not. No.

JA. Lengthening in stature was something more active and alive.

VM. Yes. And at the same time and throughout the whole business he had to keep these two things running concurrently—the speaking and the lengthening.

JA. From head to toe.

VM. From head to toe. And then he noticed that he was doing a number

---

[1] F.M. Alexander, *The Use of the Self*, Methuen, London, 1932.

of other interfering, *unnecessary*, things, with his hands, with his feet and other parts of himself—for instance, he'd actually been taught to 'take hold of the floor with his feet'—so he could see that the change he needed to make had to be a comprehensive one.

JA. And all this general interference amounted to the general shortening of stature that was ultimately conspiring to put a lot of pressure on his larynx to cause the hoarseness.

VM. That's right. Yes.

JA. It started with a stiffening and a tightening in the neck, which was the cause of the pulling back of his head, and that set off a shortening and narrowing of his whole stature.

VM. Yes. So you have to start with *not* stiffening and tightening in the neck if you're going to arrive at a lengthening of stature. Of course throughout his life he refined and clarified to himself what he was working on, but as he began to teach other people, which came quite a lot later and rather under pressure from outside . . .

JA. . . . doctors and voice trainers started sending people to him after they saw his success—since he had, in fact, cured himself of his vocal troubles through this process of self re-education.

VM. That's right. And there was, apart from the problem of the hoarseness, which was obviously primary—no voice, no career—a secondary problem, which was one of noisy breathing, which is common enough to this day among public speakers as well as the rest of us.

JA. Gasping and sucking in air through his mouth.

VM. Yes. And as he learned to maintain the lengthening of stature reliably, so that he felt he could go back on stage, when he re-presented himself, his acting colleagues wanted to know what he had been doing in the way of breathing exercises, because his breathing had so markedly improved. He told them he hadn't done any breathing exercises, but he had discovered about the lengthening of stature. The changes in his breathing had simply come about as he became successful in maintaining the lengthening. So they were eager to know what he meant, and that's how he came to show them, using his hands, what his own experience had been. But to his astonishment, nearly all of them, practically all of them, were pulling their heads back in just the same way he'd been doing, not only when they spoke, but in the beginning of practically every action.

JA. And, as I understood it, when he first tried to teach them in words alone to do what he had done, and they thought they were doing what he told them to do, he nevertheless could see that they weren't. They were still pulling their heads back and down when they thought they were telling their heads to go forward and up. Which meant that their ability to assess what was going on in themselves was as unreliable as his had been. And he deduced from that that it's an almost universal shortcoming—that nearly everyone makes errors in perception about themselves. So he saw that he couldn't teach them just through words alone, and that he had to find some way of giving them the direct feeling, the direct experience of this new and more harmonious relationship between the neck and the head and the torso that would bring about the lengthening of stature. And that's when he started using his hands to communicate it.

VM. Yes.

So Alexander, having mastered his own difficulty and having demonstrated that he had something very valuable to teach, was encouraged by his doctor friends and others to come to London, because at that time there really wasn't a big enough world in Australia for his discovery to be to recognised as the big discovery that it was. So in nineteen hundred and four he went to London, and began to work there.

JA. . . . where he not only taught many actors and distinguished people, but people from all walks of life. And he ultimately saw his technique as having the potential to help people to function as an integrated psychophysical whole—and that this had gigantic implications for the future of humanity.

VM. Yes, he really only wanted to solve his vocal problem so that he could be a better actor, and look what he found!

Then he branched out and came to the United States. He had also taught his brother to teach and sent him to maintain his practices in New York and Boston, so that there was this growing following on both sides of the Atlantic. And he was persuaded to start training future teachers in a more formal way, which he began to do in 1931, so you could say that our Alexander teaching as a profession really dates from then.

Pablo Casals teaching a master class.

F.M. Alexander giving a lesson.

XII

ALEXANDER AND CASALS

VM. So when I went to have my first Alexander lessons, my teacher simply kept stopping me doing the wrong thing, again, and again, and again, just like Casals. Don't do the wrong thing. 'Stop, stop. Remember, you need to be able to say to yourself, "Stop, and stay where you are," and then you have to ask your neck to be free in such a way that your head can go forward and up, so that your back can lengthen and widen, and this gives you the lengthening in stature, which puts you in a completely different place for arranging at the subconscious level your next action, whatever it may be.

JA. Mm. And one of the main points about Alexander's early years is that he went on refining this use of his hands to convey the experience of lengthening and to help change a person's conditions so that they could

66

much more quickly and readily feel the new integration . . . and that's basically what we call the 'Alexander Technique'—how a trained teacher uses his or her hands to convey to others this lengthening in stature and help them maintain it both in action and at rest. Which also involved releasing and reorganising the long-standing, chronic tightnesses that are usually standing in the way of the integrated working of the whole . . .

VM. . . . so we've all got into a kind of muddle, actually.

JA. Yes. And that was one of the main elements of his discovery: that even the most normal and healthy of us is in this muddle of faulty self-perception and chronic tightness, even though we don't know it—which he ultimately attributed to the rapid advancements of civilization during the last century and a half, or so.

VM. My first Alexander teacher said to me early on that 'this will increase your awareness,' and I wasn't very sure what she meant, because 'Awareness' had not yet come into fashion, though it soon did. Yet I feel that this was very much what Casals had succeeded in doing with me, through making my hearing so much more acute and awakening the sensitivity of my fingers to so much greater a degree. It didn't strike me that the two teachings were going to link up in quite the practical way they did. But I was especially intrigued by my Alexander teacher's working understanding of the anatomy and physiology. I realised I was deeply interested in that, and I thought, 'Here's the door to finding out a whole lot more about this. I have to have that knowledge if my cello teaching is going to develop.'—though the idea of becoming an Alexander teacher myself hadn't entered my head yet.

JA. Now maybe we should say something about what a traditional Alexander lesson is like.

VM. Yes. So the lessons are very often given with just a table and a chair, because in the acts of standing and sitting you are able to get right in among people's very, very deeply seated habits. And they can use the study of this action as a microcosm of everything else that they do.

JA. A paradigm for all other actions and responses in your life. And then, by working with you lying on a table, while your habits of moving and supporting yourself are at a minimum, the teacher can give you an even deeper experience of an integrated lengthening of stature that makes the chair work all the more effective when you return to it again.

VM. Yes. So you can learn an enormous amount about what Alexander termed 'inhibition' in this particular circumstance of standing up and sitting down—about being able to say 'no' to your habits—and learn a whole new 'manner of use'; how the head leads and the body follows so that the lengthening is maintained throughout the action. Nevertheless, some teachers, as mine did, will sometimes take a few moments to watch you while you put your coat on, watch you while you tie your shoes, watch you while you open the door—to see that you pay due attention to your 'manner of use' while you're doing all these things. And all that is immensely useful in making clear that the new manner of use is to be applied to everything you do all day long.

JA. And it's also important to say that in the chair work, though part of it involves the teacher guiding you with his or her hands to help you detect and prevent whatever tensions you might make that interfere with your fullest lengthening and integrating, the teacher's hands are also *giving* you an improved integration—or, at least taking you toward it, little by little, in each lesson. In fact, this is accomplished by your allowing the teacher to move you and not by doing the action yourself, while you just stay concerned with maintaining your neck-head-torso-limb directions. Then what the teacher can do with his or her hands is actually *improve* your coordination and lengthening of stature throughout the movement . . .

VM. Absolutely.

JA. . . . so that you can experience the integration in a way that can go on being achieved and improved—'progressively and endlessly,' as John Dewey wrote in his introduction to Alexander's *The Use of the Self*—no matter if you've had hundreds of lessons. So it's not only instruction you're receiving, it's also a kind of collaboration between your own self-direction and the direction of the teacher's hands.

VM. Which is a lot like Casals' playing along with me in my lessons with him. He was like a shepherd in rocky, mountain country, keeping me on the straight and narrow, and helping and encouraging me at the same time.

JA. So the music was what had to be accomplished—just like the getting out of the chair.

VM. Yes. Exactly!
As I said, in the beginning, I had no idea of the distinction between

these hundreds of notes that were not in tune and the one that was, but as I learned to distinguish I found I had an enormously increased range of possibilities, so that when the stimulus came along, when the piece required the next note, I had far, far more possibilities of supplying it appropriately—which is also what the Alexander Technique is all about. While the word integrity suggests a bringing closer together of parts to make a whole, at the same time it also gives you a vastly huger range of possible responses. And to me it's such an amazing thing that, when the bits come together, you can fly. It's the integrity that gives you the freedom. Now that I look back, I can see that Casals lengthened, he 'went up,' when he played. Because of his great integrity. And because of the high demand of the music, he was dealing with a great many stimuli all the time. So he was in a huge state of alertness that you would probably physiologically call 'excitation.'

JA. You can clearly see that integrity and alertness in the video of him giving master classes in the 1960's at Berkeley. It's so obvious.

VM. And only with this kind of integrity can you actually achieve simplicity. That's 'command!'

So it seems to me what I learned from Casals goes a long, long way along the same path with what I've learned from Alexander; I see how deep this integration was. All that stopping with Casals and saying 'no' and having to get it right every time. That was the 'chair work!' So that it isn't as if I had come to the end—absolutely not—of what I had learned from Casals, and Alexander gave me a new boost. It wasn't like that at all. The two were thoroughly enmeshed and intertwined, these two teachings. Looking back, it was rather as if I had the jigsaw puzzle, when I came back from Casals, fairly complete, but I didn't know about the head-neck-back relationship being important. Because it was all too easy for me, when I began to feel rushed and pushed by circumstances and my certainty felt threatened, to find myself watching my fingers, and so on. I even have photos of myself with my nose far too close to my fingers as I'm watching them. So when I came to Alexander, discovering the head-neck-back relationship was like finding the key piece to this puzzle.

JA. But it seems to me that Casals himself also had some idea of this overall integration that Alexander was looking for, because he's asked by Corredor in the *Conversations*[1] on page 210:

> *Do I understand that the necessary impulse to produce these flexible movements must come from the center of the body?*

[1] J. Ma. Corredor, *Conversations with Casals*, Dutton, New York, 1936.

And Casals says:

> This is, I believe, a theory entirely my own—at least no one
> ever talked to me about it, not even Monasterio. Only this
> impulse, coming from the center of the body instead of each
> extremity, will group the different movements in a unified
> whole, producing better results and less fatigue. This impulse,
> coming from what I call the center of the body, is rather like an
> image of what I feel at the time, not an easy thing to identify or
> to name.

This shows that he understood what needed to happen inside himself
when playing; and, as you say, in sitting opposite him at lessons, some of
it must have come through to you.

VM. Yes. Sometimes he would pat his heart in trying to convey something to me; which could have meant: 'from the center,' just as much as
'with feeling.'

JA. You could also say, couldn't you, that Casals was just as great an
innovator in cello playing as Alexander was in the use of the self as a
whole, in terms of how they liberated themselves from conventional as-
sumptions?

VM. Yes. I remember Casals telling us a story about the teacher he had
when he was eleven years old, Josep Garcia. Obviously, Casals was already very aware of what was helpful to himself and what was not, and
he simply refused to do what he knew to be wrong. In the *Conversations*
(p. 24) he describes it wonderfully. He says:

> My teacher was a very gifted cellist; he had good fingers, not
> too thin or too thick, which helps for fingering. Bearing in
> mind the technique and style of cello playing at that period,
> one could say he was an excellent cellist. Nevertheless, even at
> the first lesson I was very disturbed by all sorts of queer and
> conventional things which seemed absurd to me. Although I
> followed the classes quite diligently, I started revising his in-
> structions, and *as soon as I got home I created a technique of
> my own.* When the others noticed my way of playing they
> used to say: 'What are you doing? You will catch it for this.'
> But that did not stop me. I wanted to get rid of all the unnec-
> essary conventions and stiffness, which, to my mind, did not
> help to solve the real problems. [My italics. VM]

And Corredor says:

> *It sounds incredible: you were elaborating a new technique of the cello when you were twelve—a technique which in later years was to spread all over the world!*

And then Casals replies:

> Why incredible? Don't you think that even a child can observe and think what he likes of his teacher and notice what may be wrong in his teaching? We were taught to play with a stiff arm and obliged to keep a book under the armpit! What rhyme or reason is there in such an idea? I've always advocated complete freedom in the movement of the right arm, including the elbow (this new theory caused a *furore* among the traditionalists). This free action makes the whole bow technique stronger and easier.
>
> I also undertook to revise the method of fingering and the action of the left hand, keeping to my 'natural' line of approach and observation of life and nature, which can always teach us anything, if we are prepared to observe with patience and humility.
>
> These researches and thinking on technique that I started then still continue: and they will for as long as I have the strength to do so.

You know, the *Conversations* were being written while I was studying with him, but I truly don't see that these 'new methods' of Casals have reached—have infused—the teaching that I witness today. Very few string players seem to have any idea of the essence of what he possessed and how he taught it.

JA. Which, after all, is what we're hoping to convey something of in these conversations.

XIII

MORE LINKS

VM. I learned two or three other very, very important things from Casals which seem to me to show what I mean. One was when I was going up to a high D, and I missed it; he said, 'You do not know where D is?', and it was obvious that I didn't, and I had to say, 'Apparently not.' He said, 'Please, let us find D.' So we found D between us, and we played D. We played it together for quite a bit of time till we got the two D's absolutely beautifully matched. There again, my ears were being stretched and stretched. And we found D, and it was satisfactory, so we filled the room with it and we let it just percolate through the pores of our skin, as well as through our ears and eyes and our noses. We washed in this D; and we drank and soaked in it. ('D for Two!') Then he said—and he must have stopped playing his own D, because he said—'So. This is where D is, hmm?' and he swept his right hand all the way up from his left fingertip on D to his shoulder. So suddenly it became clear that he was telling me that my *arm* can know where D is . . . not just my arm, but all *that* can know where D is. It isn't just in my head. It isn't just in my ear. My brain doesn't have to tell my finger where to go; my finger can tell my brain where D is.

JA. It isn't just a point on the fingerboard.

VM. No. It's not just a point on the fingerboard. It's a relationship of me to the fingerboard. That was it. In fact, I hadn't thought of it so clearly as that—until your saying, 'It isn't just a point on the fingerboard.' It's a relationship of all of me to that spot on the fingerboard. That was very, very important. Then he said, 'Now you know where D is, let us go there.' So we went there, straight there from anywhere—no problem, straight there. For now I knew where D was. And he said, *'If you know where you are going, the journey is no problem.'* So that lesson had that outcome, that punch line, you see: if you know where it is, getting there is no problem. That cleared up a lot of mess and gave me a new point of view, a new way to practise. No more drudging up and down the finger-board, up and down, practising the journey, and still not finding where D, or C, or F actually *is*. So that was one of Casals' lessons that seemed to me to be very 'Alexander-like'—there was a kinaesthetic element. And along with that was the idea that if you know where the note is, you don't interfere, you simply go there.

Also on this kinaesthetic experience level, there was another incident of a rather different sort. It was at the very end of my time in Prades, and I'd got extremely tired. I'd got so tired that I couldn't practise at all; and I tried to explain to Casals that I couldn't practise and that I was finding it all very difficult. But he couldn't understand this because I was playing so well, and I remember doing the Brahms F Major Sonata in half a lesson on two days' practice or something, and he said 'We've done this before.' I said, 'No, no we haven't,' and I realised that by then I was working on 'capital.' I was feeling so overdone because I'd taken in as much as I possibly could take. And that was making me really rather ill. Then one day in a lesson he was sitting opposite me as usual, and he said, 'Don't use your second finger on that note, use your first.' And I could hear his words, and I could repeat them to myself, but they made no sense at all. So I thought, 'I'm going to have to ask him to play me that again.' He played it again and said, patiently, 'Not second finger, first finger.' And I couldn't make any sense of it, so I thought, 'Now if I watch him like a hawk, if I use my eyes instead of my ears, maybe I can get it.' So he did it again and he said, 'Not second finger, first finger.' And I saw quite clearly, but when I took my eyes away, the image had gone and I still couldn't make sense of it. So he began to be a little perturbed, because I wasn't usually slow like this—though he was nothing like so perturbed as I was. I was getting pretty worked up and excited and unhappy about this, when he reached over and touched the finger that I was to use. Then I knew at once, and then it was all right.

JA. That's amazing that he would think to do that!

VM. Thank goodness he did. After that, we just went on as usual. I suppose that was a kind of momentary 'nervous breakdown'—a breakdown in the nervous system.

JA. Something became disconnected.

VM. Yes. There was a failure in the connection between the intention and the muscular mechanisms—and I attribute that just to a state of total exhaustion, which is absolutely to be avoided *at all* costs. I felt that if I had to push myself any more, I'd be giving handfuls of my own flesh and blood, my substance, and nobody should ever get to that state.

JA. No. It has to be very dangerous. And that was just towards the end of your third year?

VM. Yes. Within just a few weeks I should say. At the end; in that last batch of lessons.
  And there were other very important lessons from Casals that seemed to chime with the stuff I was hearing from my Alexander teacher. For example, when I came back to England, I was doing a recital with a distinguished musician whom I'd not previously known, and he asked me, 'Could you say, in a sentence, what was the biggest single thing you learned from Casals?' I said, "Oh, Goodness, I'd have to go and think about that for a year!' But then, almost immediately, I thought 'Yes, I *can* say what it was. It was that I must be, in my entire being, right here, with what I'm doing *now*.' That is to say, there is no attention to spare for what has gone before, and there is no attention to spare for what is coming next. Even if 'now' is the middle part of a very short semiquaver, that's where my whole attention must be. It was that I needed to be 'living in the present,' if you'd like to use a very simple phrase. A dangerously popular phrase, but a rather major undertaking. This seems to be

exactly what Casals was talking about. It came about in one of my lessons when he said to me, 'What can you do about the next note while you are playing this one?' And when I considered it, I saw that there was nothing that could be done, not without a diminution of attention to this note, now; so I learned to wait and wait and wait and wait until—'*Now*!' You know when it's time. I call that 'inhibition,' in Alexander terms. And then I became—having had my ears stretched and pulled and refined in this way—so aware, that by the end of my last year with Casals, I was listening to one of my colleagues playing something he wanted me to hear, and I could hear where his attention was. I could hear when it wandered from what he was doing 'Now.' Before the end of a phrase his attention would wander off to what was coming next, and his bow would be just going along there on the string, playing a note with nothing in it.

JA. Yes.

VM. And so you also have to have your attention on the rests. Of course people pick me up on all that and say, 'Well, are you not to think ahead at all?' And I say, 'Absolutely not.' Of course you know what's coming, because you are traveling along a known pathway to a known destination. You know what the next step is *like*, but you don't *take* the next step while you're taking this step. The brain can't do it, can't accommodate it. Incidentally, when I got back to London after my first year away, and I hadn't seen a note of music for nine months, I was invited by old friends to go and read through some chamber music. And they said, 'My goodness! How your sight-reading has improved!' I used to think that the only way to improve sight-reading was to do more of it and certainly not to *not look* at the printed page for nine months! . . .

XIV

HERE AND NOW

VM. . . . so 'there's nothing you can do about what's coming next.'

JA. Which is of course what's really being taught with the Alexander Technique by using the seemingly mundane action of thinking about getting out of a chair. Just in learning to contend with that *one* proposition in a non-habitual way, you also begin to see that in practically everything else you do throughout the day, you're not really in the 'now' either. Your *thought* of what might be coming next usually causes you to get prepared for it in such a way that sabotages what needs to happen first— 'now'—in order for the best response to occur when the critical moment to act finally arrives, as when you finally get out of the chair.

VM. That's what I thought when this idea of getting out of the chair and 'not doing anything about it' was presented to me in my first Alexander lesson, 'This is meat and drink to me—child's play! I know all about that!'

JA. Yes, yes!

VM. And I suppose that the chief thing that struck me then was—that I knew all about being 'here,' 'now,' from my experience with Casals. And then, with Alexander of course, I did, as you say, realise that it applies to everything you do all day long, as well.

JA. Yet when it came to your first several attempts at being guided in and out of a chair by the teacher, did you find, like almost all beginning Alexander pupils,[1] that you were perhaps not as much able to stay in the present moment as you thought you were?

VM. Oh, yes, yes, yes! My 'chair' habits were as strong and fixed as anyone's!

But that was in spite of the fact that when I was playing B for instance, waiting to go to B flat, I had got it into my system to be 'here,' 'now.' I think I'd really learned a tremendous lot from Casals, willy nilly, about the focus of attention, and I learned a lot from him that I'm just uncovering now, as I go on giving Alexander lessons and increasingly work with musicians. For instance, the very fundamental notion of the 'whole body' being involved in playing. Because he actually said so little, the things Casals put into words stand out. I remember when he said, 'but it is all elastic!' and 'with life! with energy! but with elasticity! Eh? Eh?'—his gestures showed that he meant the whole body. And as I think I've said before, this was a new notion—that we are actually made of elastic substance—even bone is elastic, after all, to someone who knows physics.

JA. When he said that to you, did that make you try to watch him in a different way? Or did it cause you to notice that he, in fact, had that elasticity in himself when he played?

---

[1] John Dewey, the great American philosopher and educationist who studied with Alexander for many years and wrote introductions to three of Alexander's books, said of his early lessons, 'I had the most humiliating experience of my life, intellectually speaking. For to find that one is unable to execute directions, including inhibitory ones, in doing such a seemingly simple act as to sit down, when one is using all the mental capacity which one prides himself upon possessing, is not an experience congenial to one's vanity.' From Dewey's Introduction to *The Use of the Self*, p. xvii.

VM. I never looked at anything but his hands. I never consciously looked at the whole of him. As I've said, I had to watch what he was doing all the time opposite me, and I had to copy this fingering-in-the-mirror, or whatever. So I was pretty much glued to the 'business end' of Casals, which was his hands.

JA. But it never occurred to you to consider the larger notion that his total pattern of co-ordination might be at the root of whatever special ability he had?

VM. Dear me, no. I was too busy getting on with the job to wonder about anything like that. And what's more, you see, when he would get up from the cello and shuffle off to the other room, there was no beautiful lightness of step, or anything like that—no special grace.

JA. You'd notice a difference between him at the cello and when he stood up and walked about?

VM. I don't think I ever thought, 'Isn't it funny that he shuffles off to the next room like an old man, yet he plays like a young lion!' No, I wasn't aware of any discrepancy. I was just aware of his lively mind.

JA. Yes, yes. Always?

VM. Oh, yes. The attention, my goodness, the attention that I got was like a searchlight.

JA. So it wasn't until much later then, after you'd actually had Alexander lessons, that it occurred to you that he had in him what Alexander is seeking to impart to people and restore in them in terms of integration and co-ordination and psychophysical wholeness?

VM. I would never in a hundred years have thought of the phrase 'psychophysical wholeness,' I must say! Especially in thinking of someone such as Casals, who is able to make himself, when he's playing, absent, totally absent—there's nothing to look at! Perhaps 'absence' is the sublime form of 'presence!' But you can only 'absent yourself,' I would guess, if your integration is pretty well total.

JA. Absolutely.

VM. Then about his fingerings, you see. I did realise he was onto something quite extraordinary because the fingerings he used were so crazy. In the beginning I thought, 'This is completely mad.' But I found that the crazy fingerings worked. On one occasion I said, 'I don't finger this bit like that,' and he asked me to show him my fingering. It sounded pretty horrible, so he said, 'Now try this.' I did it his way, and it was good, and he said, 'Well?' No more to be said. There wasn't anything I liked better in my way than his.

JA. While we're still fairly close to the subject of Alexander, can you say when it was that it occurred to you that what Alexander discovered was something that in some way or another Casals understood or perhaps possessed in some natural way?

VM. I don't remember exactly when it was. But I do remember when I came across Lorca's essay on 'duende'[1] twenty years later, I thought, 'Of course, that's what Casals has got.' I'd felt from the beginning that Casals had got earth in his blood. Lorca says, 'duende comes up from the ground.' There was this tremendous connection with the ground in Casals, as if he came up out of the ground. I think it was sort of something that came up through his feet. And it came 'U,' 'P,' UP! You know? And I think that's what I heard when I listened to his Bach recordings and it frightened me off.

JA. Yes!

VM. He said in his *Conversations* with Corredor, that he had been blessed with a particularly good nervous system, and that I think I *could* see. But playing the cello had always been a very mental matter for me; I had never thought, 'My body is involved in this,' or that the ground had anything to do with it. And then I was put in touch with my fingertips.

JA. Yes.

---

[1] Frederico Garcia Lorca, 'Play and Theory of Duende,' in *In Search of Duende,* ed. Christopher Maurer (New Directions, New York, 1998), pp. 48-62.

XV
FINGERINGS

VM. I must have been in touch with my fingers while I was having so much success as a youngster, but I'd lost contact with them at some point during my schooldays—which must have accounted for some of the muddle. And now I see players, from time to time, with hands that I hardly recognise as hands at all. They look like an assemblage of fingers that don't belong to each other, each of which had been trained to do the same strong job. It can be a very disturbing thing to look at a hand like that, because it doesn't have the proper shape. It was obvious, working with Casals—when he was giving me the stuff about 'but elastic!' and 'natural!' and all that—that he regarded the hand as a family of fingers, each with a different role. There's a strong first finger and a pair of middle fingers that like to hang around together a bit; a big capacity for stretch between the first and second fingers; and a surprisingly strong little finger . . . and this is how he organised his fingering. He didn't try to make the fingers do what they don't like to do. So his fingers were a bunch of individuals, and he fingered accordingly, so that each one was doing what it was good at—for which it was best fitted—and that resulted in those *extraordinary* fingerings.

Another wonderful thing, which I didn't discover until much later when I'd had some anatomy training, was about the physiology of stretch. Casals knew that stretching, leaping fingerings were very good. He knew that they were more accurate. Sometimes when I was confronted with these colossal kangaroo capers, I'd say, "Why this?' and he'd say, 'Because it's safer,' and he was always right. But it always seemed so much more dangerous at first than the familiar moving 'en bloc.' And I was showing some of these fingerings one day to Don Burton [anatomy instructor in the Alexander teacher training class] when he was having cello lessons with me during our Alexander training, and I said, in passing, 'They seem to be more accurate and more sensitive, but I don't understand why.' And he said, 'But *I* do! You see, a muscle with a degree of stretch on it is sending more information to the brain!'

JA. Aha! Yes. . . and stretch also translates in Alexander terms as lengthening.

VM. Well, isn't it?

JA. Yes. But don't we need to explain that the kind of stretch we're talking about here isn't just 'stretching muscle out as far as it can go,' which usually just stimulates the reflexes that cause it to contract back more tightly than before when you stop 'stretching it out'?

VM. Yes. It's not stretch for its own sake. This is the elastic 'bound and rebound' that occurs when you jump from one stepping-stone to another. In jumping, you make practical and immediate use of the information that the stretching muscle gives you.

One of the other seminal lessons that I had from Casals was when he said, 'You see, in the tip of each finger'—and he didn't know how to say it in English, so he said it in French—'there is a "succursale" ["branch office"]—of the brain.' I got this picture of actual brain tissue in my fingertips, and this was a new idea altogether—that my *fingers* could *know*! And when he had awakened my attention by sweeping his own right hand up his left arm, the day we found D, he was paving the way for this new realisation. The finger can actually select the spot, and you don't have to do it up there at 'head office.' You may let your fingers take responsibility. And for a short but glorious period I found that I was really experiencing this. *They* knew where to go. I didn't have to do any overseeing at all. They are grown-up fingers, after all! They went about their business without Nanny, and that's what we want.

JA. Yes.

VM. And there is only one finger in operation at each time (except when you're playing double stops), and that's the one you are currently using *now*. Whether you're on a long, long note or a tiny, tiny one—there's only one finger operating *now*. And then when it's time to play the next note, the next finger takes responsibility from *now* and chooses the next place. So each finger, separately, all the way from the brain, makes its decision.

JA. Yes.

VM. And the new finger doesn't work only in relation to the note that's just been played. It isn't just my second finger stretching away from my first by an inch or two. Neurologically speaking, it's my first communicating all the way up to my brain and all the way down again from my brain to my second finger. And I experienced that very clearly when I was studying with Casals.

JA. Did he ever talk much in terms of the nervous system as such?

VM. No, the only thing he ever said about the brain or about the nervous system or about kinaesthetic experience was what I've told you, about running his right hand up his left fingers and arm, and then saying that there was a branch of the brain in each fingertip. He in some way indicated that the finger itself could know and be able to select the spot where the next note lay. And I think the grasping of that thought brought about a corresponding realisation that my fingerboard has, embedded in its length, all the notes that there are, and my business is to *choose* from what is *already there*. I'm not striking out randomly, hoping to find a match for something that I'm already hearing in my head. There's a mutuality of appeal between the note and the searching capacity of the finger. It's 'beacon' to 'beacon.' It's not just going out into the dark with a flashlight hoping you'll find what you want.

XVI

A JOINT ADVENTURE
IN ALEXANDER/CELLO

JA. This reminds me of the way you started giving me cello lessons by first showing me how to find the note a fifth above each open string—which was so easy when you showed me how I could slide my thumb down along the back of the neck of the cello as far as it would go until it hit the curve in the neck, and then the first finger very naturally ended up at the fifth, where I could also reach easily with my ring finger to the octave note halfway down the string which I could also play clearly as a harmonic by just touching lightly. And then we found our way to notes all over the instrument from that basic orientation, even very quickly going into thumb position, and easily sliding, gliding, and jumping back and forth between notes long distances apart—completely avoiding the usual static progression of learning from first position, second, third, etc. and spending a long time getting familiar with *each* of those over weeks or even months . . .

VM. . . . or even a year! . . .

JA. . . . before moving on to the next in an ever more static way. And I remember the complete kinaesthetic thrill of it all—just being able to jump and bound all over the fingerboard like that, getting right into the DeFesch sonata very early on and mainly approaching it from the larger gestures involved in the phrases rather than from painstakingly learning it one note at a time. And then we got to *The Swan* fairly soon after that too, I think, which seems to demand a lot more variety in playing than most first year string students ever learn.

VM. I think *The Swan* is a Grade VII piece! You take a few years to reach Grade VII!

JA. Oh! I know I certainly couldn't have begun to play anything that advanced on violin even after having a whole year of string class every day back in college—taught by a wonderful cellist, I might add, and assisted by an excellent upperclassman violist too.

And maybe the most exciting of all was when you had me play the first B on the A string with my first finger, and keep on playing it while you took my little finger and stretched it way back toward the scroll like we were aiming a sling shot—already having shown me the spot way down the string where the G we were aiming for was—and then *boing*, you let go, and my fourth finger *flew* down there, leading all the rest of my hand with it in a very natural way! It seemed all the more astonishing because you were actually taking my fourth finger farther and farther *away from* where it ultimately was going to land; and if you'd asked me to try to get to the G by myself from the B, I'm *sure* I would have been somehow preparing in my fingers, hand and arm mainly to reach *toward* it, which of course would have taken my attention away from playing the B. And now, from all you've been saying, I see that you were really starting me out on cello with all the things that would develop the elasticity and the connection of brain to fingertips. So were these approaches to teaching ones that you gleaned from working with Casals or ones that you've developed on your own since then?"

VM. I wouldn't say 'gleaned,' because to me that suggests a rather effortful sifting for good stuff among rather scanty pickings, when what I got from Casals was a bountiful harvest! I've devised a few games and exercises, but I didn't feel I needed to invent much.

I'm delighted to hear you say, 'the sheer kinaesthetic thrill of it.' Hooray! That's what I'd most like my pupils to get, for the pleasure and the sense of, 'I can do it!' and the fearlessness—all of which puts you in the best possible state for going adventuring in a new skill. Because there you were, gadding about all over the place and getting into the DeFesch and *The Swan* from what you felt were the 'larger gestures involved in the phrase,' and *yet*, you were also getting a very high degree of accuracy—I wouldn't have allowed you *not* to. So you're right, I wanted you to start with the elasticity and the connection of brain to fingertips; but I wasn't *planning* to bring you to a high state of excitement. But of course excitation of a physiological sort would obviously be the result, and with that a sparkling alertness. The security would obviously just drop into place.

I didn't start you out with one note at a time, as Casals did with me, because his work was remedial; and I was wanting you to be at home on the cello. You see, you weren't the first professional musician that I started on the cello. My husband, Gordon, was the first, before we were married. He was a conductor, and he wanted to know more about cello playing by doing some. My aim with him was to give him what he needed to get about the cello, and he too gave a very good account of *The Swan*—on the only twelve lessons he had with me. After we were married there were no more cello lessons, but I used to hear him grappling with the Beethoven sonatas—so he *had* learned enough to get about on his own. Aim accomplished! He had had some systematic violin teaching, like you, from a first rate teacher, but he said he never felt capable of going further on his own. With you though, I was finding out how to teach the cello 'on Alexander lines,' and, as you knew more about Alexander than I did because you were a whole year ahead of me in the teacher training, I felt I had to be extra vigilant. And I've always supposed you were also finding out about learning something new from the Alexander perspective. All that made giving you lessons hugely valuable for me.

XVII

MORE LINKS . . .

JA. But what was it mainly that you felt you needed to learn from the Alexander Technique to be able to use in your cello teaching?

VM. Well, Casals had given my cello playing a new basis—elasticity was paramount—and I had found that the risktaking and the trust in the fingers' own intelligence led to accuracy by so different and so much more *reliable* a route—not to mention the excitingness. Here, in the Alexander Technique, I could see I was going to find a ratification of that physiologically and acquire a knowledgeable foundation from a different angle—for everything I tackled—so that I could go forth with a reliable map and compass, rather than having *only* an overwhelming cello experience to work from. My Alexander teacher also seemed to embody an anatomical and physiological understanding that I realised I was thirsting for.

JA. But wasn't it also that you saw that you might be able to gain further expertise in helping your cello students experience more within the overall kinaesthetic realm of the use of the self as a whole too?

VM. Yes. There was the day, for instance, when I 'discovered' my back for the first time and had the experience of its beginning to work. I could see there was a lot of strength and power there to be developed in this subtle Alexander way. Other cello teachers occasionally mentioned the back. You know, 'Your bowing, dear, starts in the back.' Well, just being told that doesn't really mean very much . . . .

JA. Like just *telling* a nervous or tense player they need to 'relax.'

VM. Exactly—even when the cello teacher touches you between the shoulder blades and says, 'That's where your bowing comes from,' as I remember my teacher did to me. I wanted to be able to help my pupils a great deal more than that. And to show them convincingly that it's from the whole back that the bowing comes, all the way down to the chair.

JA. You saw that a good Alexander teacher can often give you the experience of the working of your back in a way that's actually linked up with your hands and arms, and that they can also teach you how to maintain it.

VM. Yes. And I thought, 'I can't possibly be teaching anyone to use their hands to play the cello without their having this experience of themselves as a whole.' As I said, I began to be 'put in touch with my "body,"' as they say these days. Or rather, I could say this experience provided a fuller and more *accurate* sense of being in touch, because I believed I already was 'in touch with my body' through dancing.

JA. Yes.

VM. I loved dancing. I used to spend hours dressing up in ballet frocks I made from my mother's curtains, and I really fancied myself as the next Isadora Duncan, like lots of little girls. But besides that, I've always enjoyed the movement that music obliges you to make when you're playing the cello.

JA. Yes.

VM. I enjoy the sweeps of the bow and the springiness of the strings, and all that as a kind of dance thing. Those gut strings make a wonderful trampoline—the more you throw the bow at them the more they bounce you off.

JA. Yes!

VM. As I think I've said before, one of Casals' favourite phrases was, '*Do only what is necessary*' one of the big revelation phrases. Now that's also an Alexander type utterance. We're not going to handle a lot of extras, we're going to do a simple, straight-forward, 'what-it-takes-to-do-it' job. And 'what is necessary' will be all you need. And I found that often doing what was necessary meant doing a great deal *more* than I had ever done before. A *great deal* more. Sometimes, doing only what was necessary meant doing a great deal less.

All of what I learned with Casals seemed to go in two directions. It seemed to be taking me in one direction, but it also took me in the opposite direction. More freedom leading to more accuracy, for instance. Both good. It was a tremendous stretch beyond my previous limits. So a tremendous lot *more* was sometimes necessary, and this very necessity put me through some marvelous kinaesthetic experience. I'd always enjoyed all that, and when I began to teach cello, as soon as I came back from Casals, I found out inadvertently how surprisingly little some people are aware of what they're actually doing when they play, and how little they enjoy the feel of it. And how the rhythm often exists only in their heads or in their tongue and teeth or foot as they count '1, 2, 3, 4.' But it doesn't pervade their whole being as I feel it does in me.

JA. Yes.

MORE LINKS . . .

XVIII

INTO RHYTHM

VM. I suppose you could call it, you know, the animal nature of rhythm.

JA. Don't you think that in some people that whole-self response to rhythm or pulse is not available because of their poor use of themselves; and when they try to play something more musically, this availability to move, or to 'dance,' is blocked? Then they go to seek out eurythmics or some other 'movement' training to try to access it.

VM. Yes! I think it's not only their poor use of themselves, but often ill-conceived technique that puts their natural elasticity out of reach. For instance, when the hand is all bunched up, and the fingers are used like little hammers, that creates a block of tightness that deprives the brain of the stretch information which allows the rest of the body to give full play to this natural animal rhythm.

JA. Yes. I guess that's what we were really invoking that day in your singing lesson with Angela Caine. Do think it's worth describing here—since it was so exciting?

VM. Yes, I do . . . .

JA. It was back in '83 when I was visiting London for some refresher Alexander lessons and you asked me to come to your singing lesson and work on you during it. You'd been collaborating for some time with Angela doing singing/Alexander weekend courses, so you knew she'd understand why you wanted me there to work on you in your lesson. And I guess she must have been just as curious as you were to see what might happen.

VM. Yes, I know I was all agog to have the chance of being 'worked on' experimentally in the sort of way I was doing on those weekend courses—and it was thrilling and effective beyond my best hopes! Go on.

JA. As I remember, it was in a large room where you two had just been giving a singing class to some Alexander students. I know I didn't have any idea of what I might be able to do with the Technique to help, and you didn't ask me to do anything in particular either—other than just 'work on' you in whatever way I saw fit. So we just started in. You were singing Mahler's *Songs of a Wayfarer*, and Angela was accompanying you on the piano and keeping an eye on us too to see what we were doing.

Somehow I knew that I just couldn't follow the conventional Alexander teacher's approach to working with performers and leave you standing there in one spot singing while I gave you neck, head, trunk directions with my hands, because I knew it would be too static and dull—even though it *might* have helped to free things up some and improve your overall integration enough to enhance your breath support and general *vocal* quality—not that I had ever heard you sing and could estimate what you might need.

But since I knew the *Songs of a Wayfarer* fairly well too and couldn't help responding to their feeling and rhythm myself, I realised I wanted to use my hands on you in a way that would be a part of the expression of the music—almost as much as it would be if I were playing or singing it myself. So I just started moving you with my direction, with no words at

90

all, in whatever ways that I could let the musical flow of each phrase take us. Sometimes it was merely taking you into a few steps with a phrase, but it also could turn into my bending and torsioning you, or maybe only moving your arms. I wasn't thinking of it in any way as 'dancing,' yet to an observer it must have looked almost like a kind of reserved *pas de deux,* since my own moving was 'with the phrase' at the same time. But there wasn't any choreographic intention in it at all, because I wasn't consciously 'choosing' how to move myself and you in terms of creating any visual effect. Also, I don't think it's something I would have been able to do if I hadn't done a lot of spontaneous improvisational moving or dancing to music *myself* all my life—as you just told me you'd done too.

So I wasn't merely trying to 'help you with your singing by working on you with the Technique.' I was participating in the musical expression almost as much as you and Angela were as you produced the actual sound. And the difference in your singing was incredible.

VM. Yes! But you know, I have the most vivid recollection of what happened, and it's quite different from yours. I remember you very gently putting a finger under each of my armpits at the back, and that got me widening. Then you gently lifted my chin a little—which was astonishing—and I began to feel like a tube full of voice. I didn't have to think about breathing or anything else. And every now and then you had me walking a step backwards; so it felt like a *pas de deux* to me too, but we covered *very* little ground. I remember your hands encouraging me to twist and turn in the gentlest fashion—what you call 'torsioning.' Each time, your hands seemed to find just the right thing to do to keep it all going—quite masterly! And I remembered all the words, which was amazing, because I don't usually. So the remembering of the words comes from the coordination of the whole—but that's not where we go looking for the words when we can't find them, is it? But I think, all in all, everything that you were doing was, in fact, reinforcing the animal rhythm, so that it became clear that that was the unifying factor. As Casals used to say, 'But it's the rhythm!'

JA. Don't you think that, because we'd also played a certain amount of chamber music together and were generally on the same wave length musically, it happened more easily than it might have with someone else?

VM. Oh, yes!

JA. What do you think of the idea of trying to educate rhythmic skills through specific (and separate) movement education?

VM. Well, I think good Dalcroze training can be wonderful. My one class with Valerie Roth in Paris was a revelation. But then Dalcroze is more of a comprehensive musical training and not limited to movement. I think that if you've got a good music teacher, separate 'movement' training shouldn't be necessary. Looking back, I feel that almost from the beginning our musical training was wanting in wholeness. The emphasis was so much on getting on, in terms of exams and grades and so on, and all in so much of a hurry. Then when I came back from Casals, I told people with amazement and delight and revelation written all over me that I had spent three months on the first three lines of the Haydn. They said, 'Oh, nobody teaches that way nowadays.'

JA. 'Who could be bothered to take that long on so little?'

VM. Yes, and 'Weren't you bored to death?' was another very common reaction. These two typical reactions came up again and again. And the third, which I only surmised, was, 'My goodness, she must have been dim to have to spend three months on three lines of the Haydn!' So I stopped telling people how Casals had me work. I really did. Because they didn't understand. (And yet it was this very minutely careful work that was putting me in touch with the quintessential animal rhythm.) A few people who had been to him for lessons told me that they didn't understand what he was talking about as a teacher. And I have to feel that this was the most magnificent teaching ever.

JA. Yes!

VM. Because it was always, and only, attending to what was necessary.

JA. Yes! But don't you also think that the 'quintessential *animal* rhythm' is something more than, or even something *beyond*, the mere 'rhythmic skill' that's usually considered the basic requirement of all good musicianship—even though animal rhythm would certainly show itself largely through your regular rhythmic skills?

VM. Oh, yes—'animal' itself is too limited a word. That boat on the sea
. . .

JA. Yes. I feel there's an additional element that I somehow want to call the 'pulse' or the 'impulse' of a phrase that can also exist without particularly tying it down to any steady beat. But maybe it's more the same thing you mean by 'pace' as distinct from tempo, which is about the 'coming and going' of notes and phrases that you said you thought Casals exemplified so fully.

92

VM. Yes, the boat on the sea. The wind and the tides between them must provide an infinite range of ever-changing influences—an oceanic rhythm—and even when something enormous and catastrophic occurs, like a volcanic eruption under the sea, the tidal wave that comes after, even though it totally overwhelms the boat, is still encompassed by, is still a part of, the ebb and flow that's inherent in all living things.

JA. Yes! That reminds me of what Susanne Langer says about the essence of rhythm in music and how in the organic unity of the physiological rhythms of our breathing and our hearts beating—the systole and diastole—we can sense 'a beginning, intent, and consummation, and see in the last stage of one the condition and indeed the rise of another . . . rhythm is the basis of life.'[1] And I think a lot of what we're talking about here could actually be the root of real 'musicality'—as distinct from 'musicianship'—and that 'real musicality' and 'animal rhythm' are maybe one and the same. And a person with no musical training whatever can possess it—even more so sometimes than someone with a full conservatory background.

VM. Yes, I'm afraid I think the 'full conservatory background' can be the death of all sorts of natural feeling and impulse. But it may still be possible to get it back.

JA. And when we were tapping into that more natural feeling and impulse in your singing lesson, it wasn't just because I was 'moving you rhythmically with some Alexander directing behind it.' I could easily have done that, but it would have been an entirely different experience and one I'm pretty sure you'd have found a gross interference with your own animal rhythm.

VM. Yes. I'd probably have wanted to kick and spit—though I've certainly done things like that to many a performer. I'm glad they haven't kicked or spat. What we got to that day was something very profound, to do with the circulation of the lymph or something even more visceral. All you can do when you've got to that layer is to lie low and just not interfere—it will carry on of its own accord. That's a really awesome experience.

JA. Yes. And with Casals, for instance, on the recording of him rehearsing the Brandenburg concertos with the Marlboro Festival Orchestra, sometimes he'll give the first beat of a segment he's rehearsing with a

[1] Susanne K Langer, *Feeling and Form*, pp. 126-127, Charles Scribner's Sons, New York, 1953.

great, loud stomp of his foot and then a yell at the moment the instruments are supposed to enter. But the *way* he stomps—just that once! There's a life and vitality in it that goes way beyond merely supplying the players with an accurate and energetic first beat so that they can make their entrance correctly in time. It's as if the stomp contains in it the whole essence of that particular movement of the concerto, and if you only heard—and *felt*—that one stomp, that'd be enough to understand the whole allegro movement. And I would think that 'duende' would be in that stomp too—and that it wouldn't necessarily be the kind of thing you'd learn from the rhythmic training most of us have when it's just clapping your hands or tapping your pencil on your desk to the various note-values. I know that if I were playing in that orchestra under him at that moment, that foot stomp would electrify my own animal rhythm in a stupendous way, beyond anything my regular rhythmic skills contained. Even just listening to it on the record inspires every cell in me to want to move—even if only just to jump up out of my chair or throw my arm up into the air.

VM. Bravo! What a wonderful description! That's the other end of the spectrum that brings us full circle—and does away with any idea of measuring.

I heard a wonderful young violinist start off a performance of his east European 'folk' group by jumping in the air and coming down with a stomp just like that, with both feet, and that set the whole piece rolling right on to the end. *That's* what a musical education should do for you! He told me he always felt nervous performing in a music college and that it had taken him years to shake off the influence of his own conservatory training. Which is not to say it isn't necessary for us to go through it. Who was it who said 'all trainings are stiffening'?

JA. I don't know, but it seems likely to be true!

XIX

ON INTO ALEXANDER TRAINING −1970

JA. But when you encountered the Alexander Technique, you weren't content just to have lessons. You still wanted something more out of it—the skill that an Alexander teacher has—to be able to actually communicate that fuller experience of the whole self as part of your cello teaching.

VM. Early on I never thought of becoming an Alexander teacher. I just knew that here, in the Technique, was a whole lot of information and knowledge that I had to have to integrate with my cello teaching. It was very soon after I began Alexander lessons that I came to feeling that nobody should be teaching an instrument without this knowledge—this understanding—this . . . knowledge, yes . . . as an integrated part of their teaching equipment.

JA. So you didn't decide right away that you must do the three-year training course to become an Alexander teacher?[1]

VM. I hadn't got to that yet. No, I made a much bigger jump than that really. Because having decided that I had to have this knowledge if my cello teaching was going to develop—and I really was very passionately interested in teaching at that time—was a great big new idea and a big enough thing to take on board at that stage.

JA. Yes.

VM. And besides, just then I was doing very little teaching. I was very occupied with my husband and my two young boys. The next step was my thinking, 'But this is what I'd like to have *done*. I'd like to have been an Alexander teacher.' Because it's so much wider, so much deeper, so much more interesting than only being a cellist—or what being a cellist struck me as at that time.

JA. Oh, so you were thinking of it more in terms of an alternative to, rather than just a supplement to, your cello teaching?

VM. Not at all. A beyond. Not an alternative. A beyond and an expansion. It seemed to offer me ways to take what I had learned from Casals into a wider field—full of promise. And since there was no possibility, as far as I could see, of my ever doing such a thing as the teacher training, that's more or less where it rested in my own mind. I had so many other things to think about at the time.

JA. Yes.

VM. I had many other things to think about; but I did think, 'This is what I'd like to have done,' in the sense of, 'Well, what a nice idea. This is a really lovely kind of work. All sorts of new fields that I've always been interested in would open up. There's so much that this opens up.' And I had, after all, been at the cello since I was six. I had always moved

---

[1] Since 1931, the training to become a teacher of the Alexander Technique has required a minimum of three years' intensive daily study. Now the Society of Teachers of the Alexander Technique, in conjunction with the world-wide Affiliated Societies, requires a minimum of 1,600 hours for certification. A minimum of seven years' teaching experience is required before a teacher is eligible to train others to teach.

among musicians, mostly cellists, and I thought, 'Wouldn't it be nice to move out of this tight circle and meet other people?' Because when you start cello when you're six, you know, it's a big shaping of your life for a child. It cut me off from a very great deal of normality—just making me that much different.

JA. But then it did come; the possibility presented itself that you could go further in the Alexander work and train?

VM. Yes, but it happened very suddenly and quite a long time after I started private lessons, maybe a year and a half.

JA. Yes.

VM. And I suppose that meanwhile I went on having private Alexander lessons because I needed them.

JA. When the opportunity to train did arise, you immediately said, 'Yes, I'll do it.'

VM. Absolutely. There was no question about that. There were a great, great many practical difficulties, of funds, and having to move my home yet again and so on, but when I said, 'This is what I really want to do,' that was perhaps the first choice about my own life that I had ever made.

JA. Really?

VM. Yes, because, after all, I'm told the decision to play the cello was mine; but it was a decision taken at the age of six which was immediately seized upon by all and sundry; so they could say, 'Well, this is what you *said* you wanted to do!' and then they could sweep me into all those competitions and things, you know?

JA. Yes.

VM. It was certainly not an adult choice about what I would like to do with my life. It was a choice based on very little experience, obviously. At the age of six it really has to be! Of course, there were piano lessons as well. I had a lot of lovely times with music as a kid, but not on the cello. Lovely times at the piano and composing and feeling around, improvising. I did all that because *I* wanted to. Then eventually, after a certain number of Alexander lessons, I thought, 'This is what I would like to have done.' And that was a proper grown-up statement. Because even all through school, you see, you do what you're good at. And if you say you'd like to specialise in something different or unexpected, it takes nerve to insist on it, against parents' and teachers' wishes—at least in my generation. I do know someone who recently said, 'I would like to specialise in such-and-such,' naming something that she was very bad at. Nobody could understand why. She said, 'Because I'm *bad* at it, and I'd like to get better.' That seems to me very wise and sensible. So you've always sort of fumbled along, and you tend to make choices on what has already been half-decided, really. So here was this decision I'd made about the Alexander training suddenly bearing fruit—especially thrilling because I'd thought it couldn't happen. It couldn't happen, and I had rather dismissed it from my mind. With small children and no money, there's no question. However, I did write to Walter Carrington,[2] on my Alexander teacher's advice, and I had a lesson with him. And I put in writing that I would like to train if it ever became possible, to declare my interest 'officially.' So when events shifted dramatically so that I actually could join the training course, we were already halfway there.

---

[2] Walter Carrington trained with F.M. Alexander in the late 1930's, became his main assistant, and remained so until Alexander died in 1955. Since then Mr. Carrington has continued with the training of Alexander teachers, along with his wife Dilys, at the Constructive Teaching Centre, London.

ON INTO ALEXANDER TRAINING — 1970

98

XX

TO HELL AND BACK –
A THREE DAY SAGA

_JA._ But in the meantime, there's the question as to what sort of effect the Alexander work already might have had on your cello playing in the early stages before you joined the training course.

_VM._ Yes. People have often said, 'What difference did it make to your playing?' Well—quite honestly—I think my playing was extremely good at that stage!

_JA._ Yes.

_VM._ When I was first having my Alexander lessons I had no worries about my playing. Of course, it wasn't easy, it never is—but I have never wanted to have a cello lesson with anyone else. Now if you have been seventeen years without having the least desire to have a lesson with anyone else—because who do you go to after Casals? I didn't have any worries. I knew that I had enough to be going on with. When he said to me, 'There is nothing you cannot do,' I believed him. I thought, 'My goodness, he's right.' And so I set to work with the tools he'd given me. And I was fortunate in having a husband whose musical opinion I valued and trusted—which was very good. So I hadn't come anything *like* to the end of assimilating what Casals had given me to go away and use. I didn't want any other input, except the sort of corrective and appreciative input that I could get from a small succession of colleagues, culminating in my husband, who was both a keyboard expert and a conductor. So I didn't have any worries about that. But I do remember, fairly early in my Alexander lessons, doing some chamber orchestral dates and having a pretty tricky passage to play along with my fellow cellist. It went very well, and she said, 'I wish you could teach me what Casals taught you,' because I played this passage with extreme ease; and I think I'd ascribe that to the Alexander experience that I'd had so far. You see, it slipped in smoothly alongside the cello technique without there having to be any modification at all in the cello technique. It just opened it up some more and gave me more freedom. The Alexander Technique threw a new light on what I'd got from Casals, just as what I'd got from Casals illuminates what the Alexander Technique has to offer.

JA. But there was the instance that you wrote about in one of the testimonial letters from professional musicians for my master's thesis on the effects of the Alexander Technique in dealing with stress in performance,[1] when you told about the concert where I think you were playing the Haydn concerto in C, and that you attributed a lot of its success to what you had learned from your early Alexander lessons.

VM. That's a long story, you know—shall I tell you it all over again?

JA. Yes, do, because it's really great!

VM. Well, I had this concert date after about a year of Alexander lessons. A lot of very tumultuous things had been happening in my life since I had been asked to play this concerto—which was one I'd never performed before. And I was working away on it as best I could, but I was still having a few slips of memory. I had a friend who was an amateur pianist

---

[1] 'Effects of the Alexander Technique in Dealing with Stress in Musical Performance,' Tufts University, May, 1975. Available at http://www.home.earthlink.net/ ~jarmstrongatech/

who had run through it once or twice with me, and each time she did, I thought, 'My goodness, I don't remember where to come in here,' or, 'I think I may have made a wrong turn there.'

The day of the concert came nearer and nearer. I was very deeply committed to other things—other non-musical things—so that my practice time was in fact limited. But not too limited. It wasn't irresponsible of me to have undertaken to do this concert, but I was finding the whole thing rather overwhelming. It was just the difficulty of the demand and my own extreme fatigue. Well, it was two nights before the concert. I was staying in Edinburgh. Both my boys, who were six and seven, developed chicken pox. I was delighted. I said, 'I can't do the concert!' And my hostess, the pianist, said, 'Oh yes you can; we'll manage here somehow.' It was going to be extremely difficult for her to have two sick boys around the house while I was away, but something was going to be managed.

So I was pushed onto the night train to London. It was in Surrey, south of London, that I had to play. So I was pushed onto the night train, and I took a couple of sleeping pills. I made sure I slept. Then I got to London early, early, early in the morning. And I was just so consumed with nervousness and unreality that I had to make conversation with just anybody. The man sweeping the platform, 'That's a nice looking broom you've got there.' An unlikely looking down-and-out who'd been sleeping in the station. Yes, anything to talk to someone who'd keep me in touch with reality, because I was really so frightened about this whole thing that was coming nearer and nearer. So, getting a grip on myself, I thought, 'Well, I shall meet the conductor, when I get down to the station in Surrey, and he'll take me to his house, and we shall have a run-through and either he will say, 'That's all right!' (shivers) or he will say, 'Well, this is not quite up to par.' In that case, of course, I'll ask Christopher Bunting [a well-known English cellist] to come out and play it for me. It just happened that about a year before, I'd had to cancel a performance of the same concerto for quite different reasons, and Christopher had played in my place. So I thought, 'Well, I'll just ask him to do that again.' Be it noted that I hadn't thought very deeply about whether he was in the country or willing or ready or available or anything like that!—but that was my let-out—that Christopher would play it for me if I wasn't fit.

While I was at the station in London I rang up a staunch old friend as soon as it was decently late enough to speak to anyone. He said, 'Now, how are you doing?' and I said, 'Well, I'm um um um,' and I slid down the wall of the telephone booth. My legs gave way underneath me. So I straightened my legs and pushed myself up and I had this conversation.

He said, in a very firm voice, 'Now you may be able to find a chemist who will give you a bromide drink. Do that.' So I thanked him and I put every bit of my energies into getting a bromide drink out of a chemist at Waterloo station. And I succeeded. And I think it was probably a very good thing. I don't know whether the bromide drink gave any help, but it gave me something concrete to do while I waited. Because this is what is so extremely frightening—having nothing to do while you wait. And so I suppose, meanwhile, when I wasn't sliding down the wall of the telephone booth, or even when I was, I was freeing my neck and giving my directions.[2] It was hard going. And still I had this 'let-out,' you see, 'Christopher will play if the conductor says, "This won't do."'

So in due course I'd got on the train in London and went on to Surrey, and there was my friend the conductor, and he said, 'How nice to see you. I'm terribly sorry we shan't be able to have our piano rehearsal until this evening.' Then he delivered me at his home. I spent the day at his home with his wife and children, and I thought, 'Alexander Technique!' 'Now I really have to do the directing and the inhibition and the watching myself—not letting things get out of hand.' So somehow I got through that day. I did a little very disciplined practice. The conductor came home and we had our run-through with the piano. He said, 'That's terrific!' I made a couple of slips, but he still said, 'That's terrific! I have no worries about that at all.' So I thought, 'Now I'm really in for it! Eighteen hours to go! Eighteen hours.' So I think I slept that night. I don't remember not sleeping.

The next day I was exceedingly attentive, and I found that the most important thing that I had to do was to *not allow* this concerto to run around in my head unless I was there watching it. I never let it get out of hand. I never let it run away without me. In my head, I went thoroughly, in a business-like fashion, from the beginning to the end of the concerto. Once in the morning, and once in the afternoon. I had done this the day before as well. Then I said, 'Right, I will not think about that again.' And whenever I found that the music was beginning to creep into my head, I put it out. Because I was afraid that I was only doing easy bits, or perhaps that I was rehearsing my slip-ups. I couldn't be quite sure, so I didn't take any risks. 'Won't do any of that. It's a waste of time.' It plainly would be a waste of time if my attention was not fully on the music. So I eliminated all that.

---

[2] The series of ideo-kinetic self-directives the Alexander Technique teaches for facilitating and maintaining an integration of the postural mechanisms in daily life: 'neck free, head forward and up, back to lengthen and widen, knees forward and away.'

JA. It's worth saying here that this falls under the category of 'inhibiting' in Alexander practice. 'My technique is based on inhibition, the inhibition of undesirable, unwanted responses to stimuli, and hence it is primarily a technique for the development of the control of human reaction.'[3]

VM. Yes! And I did my 'whispered Ah's,' and I did my 'hands on the back of the chair,' and I did my 'lying on my back with books under my head,'[4] and altogether kept a very strict watch over everything . . . 'conscious control.'[5]

JA. Over everything—within yourself?

VM. Yes. Everything that was going on in me. I remembered my first Alexander teacher's first injunction, which was, 'Just stop all that.' And I said, 'All what?' And she said, 'You know, all that, that's going on.' Then I realised that I did know *exactly* what she meant. All these extraneous manifestations of my constant state of anxiety, which were making it impossible to be 'here, now,' and just keeping my neck free. I watched over all that. And it was so amazing because it didn't have to be analysed or given a cause or named or anything. All she had to say was, 'Just stop all that.' and I just had to think of freeing my neck. And it worked!

Then the time came for the rehearsal, and we went to the hall. I walked up the steps to the platform, and, faced with the professional orchestra, I said to myself, 'Be professional, Vivien.' We had twenty-five minutes—just about enough time for my concerto. So I smiled at everyone, and we began. By the end of the concerto I'd made two slips—not the same ones. Then I said, 'Could we just do the two bars before letter H please?' So we did. I said, 'Yes, that's all right.' And the conductor said, 'Now, just second violins, we'll do four after Q.' So we rehearsed that bit. And he said, 'All right?' and I said, 'Yes, that's all right.'

The next thing was going to be the performance. I remember it all very clearly. And I thought, 'Well, I should be able to do a little warming up in the artists' room before we start,' but in the evening when I got to the artists' room I could not so much as tune my cello, because the room was

---

[3] F.M. Alexander, *The Universal Constant in Living* (1941), Mouritz, London, 2000, p. 88.

[4] Procedures devised by Alexander to both release excessive tension and to develop a more refined control over the use of the self as a whole—particularly with regard to the working of the breathing mechanisms.

[5] F.M. Alexander, *Constructive Conscious Control of the Individual*, Integral Press, Kent, 1923.

directly underneath the platform, and the orchestra was right over my head. I couldn't risk making any noise down there, so I had to walk on pretty well cold. And I started to play, and the anxiety fell off like a cloak and lay about my feet in folds. And I just left it there, and I had nothing to do with it. I thought, 'This playing doesn't feel like me. But those are my fingers.' So I said, 'Just stop all that,' and went on playing. And it was so exciting. The supreme experience, among all my experiences, in which it simply 'happened to me' as it went by. And I think I may have made a couple of slips, but nothing that showed or mattered. I'm not even sure that I did. I was really on the ball all through that performance. And, as I say, it was very, very exciting. And there was a curious lack of fore-knowledge. As I say, it was happening *to* me. So much so that when during an orchestral tutti, I thought, 'Is this where I come in? No! It isn't. No! I wonder if it's *now*? No. No. Ah—here it is!' And I came in. I wasn't counting bars or anything. I just knew that, you know, I was as much a part of the orchestra as I was the soloist. It was like being a bare-back rider at the circus who has to jump on the right horse as the horses gallop round the ring. And it was a most extraordinary and exciting experience. At the end the audience rose to their feet. True, it was a very friendly audience, but it was a wonderful reception. And I seem to remember looking round behind me to see who they were clapping for. It was quite extraordinary. I thought, 'Gosh, that's *me* they're applauding!'

JA. And right then you had a sense that you had that triumph over all those adversities because of the Alexander work that you had done on yourself that day and the previous day?

VM. Oh, yes. Oh *yes*. And of course the improved use of myself generally would have accounted for some of it, but I have no doubt it was the desperate situation that made me really and truly apply what I'd been learning with all that was in me.

JA. Yes.

VM. I really did manage to keep at bay all the ghosts and gremlins and all the things that come in on an occasion like that. And treat the occasion as pure adventure, which I suppose means accepting what's happening with open arms and meeting it as it comes.

JA. You couldn't have come from the station in this tizzy and just told yourself, 'Oh well, just let it be an adventure, Vivien.'

VM. Oh dear me no. No, it was the strict control that allowed it to be an adventure. It was a liberating control.

JA. That you really established in yourself as a whole, then and there in that couple of days by working on yourself as you did.

VM. Yes. Because all the preconceptions and all the 'what-might-happen-if' and 'supposing-that'—all that was eliminated from my field of attention. Nothing was allowed to dribble out at the edges, you know?

JA. Yes. But a lot of people who don't know much about the Alexander Technique probably have the idea that one just has lots of lessons that somehow make one different and then later one can just automatically play with more control. But they don't realise the responsibility it takes at every moment—particularly in times of crisis.

VM. That's right. We do have a way of dealing with crisis, but it involves looking after yourself and dealing with every moment as it comes, not just relying on what has been built up with the teacher in the lessons. No, no. But I had had enough lessons to be able manage pretty well . . . though in fact, you know—here's another story—very much earlier in my lessons I was going to the dentist and I was full of fear and I said to my teacher, 'What can I do in the dentist's chair?' and she said, 'Well, you've had very few lessons so I can't guarantee anything, but of course you can try to remember to free your neck and send your head forward and up.' But I didn't only do that, I did whispered Ah's, which I'd recently been introduced to. And I dare say they were not good whispered Ah's at all. They had been well explained to me, and I think I got the hang of them quite quickly. So I did a good number of those on my way to the dentist. The fear was that I was going to have a broken tooth taken out. When I got there, he said, 'I'm not going to touch that today.' So I didn't actually have to meet that crisis, but I'd had plenty of fear to deal with in advance. When I went back to my next Alexander lesson, my teacher said, 'My goodness, what a difference there is in your back. What have you been doing?' So I said, 'Nothing special, no, nothing. But I did the whispered Ah's.' And she said, 'That's it. *That's* why your back's so much stronger.' I believed her then. I certainly believe her now that I have much more experience. But I believed her then. And I thought, 'that's remarkable.' But you see, there again, in an extreme case, I did what I had been told needed to be done, and to great effect. And it isn't just a question of thinking about something else instead. It's simply not allowing these destructive things to creep into your head at all.

JA. Yes. So fairly early on you had this experience of carrying through for yourself what you'd been learning in the Alexander lessons.

VM. During the concert I had this very stunning experience. The whole performance must have lasted seventeen minutes or so. Seventeen minutes with no mind wandering—that's quite an achievement for me. Really no 'ifs,' or 'buts'—just seventeen minutes of being in the present.

XXI

HELL ANATOMIZED –
NERVOUSNESS DISSECTED

JA. So the fear or nervousness, whether in the performance situation or any other life situation, can discoordinate one, can throw one off, so that no matter how much skill or ability one has developed in a field, like cello playing, it still can be rendered inaccessible.

VM. Yes. Fear discoordinates. You see, in spite of the years with Casals I'd had, if you put me on the concert platform, I could be as nervous as anyone else. I had no means of dealing with it except the familiar means of, you know, taking 'deep breaths,' telling yourself you're good and so on. Prayer even . . .

JA. And, of course, didn't Casals himself even say that the very thought of a concert still made him nervous—even late into his career?

VM. Oh yes, he did.[1]

JA. Had nervousness been much of a problem with you all along?

VM. I think I became more nervous as I grew up—nervousness is infectious anyway, and it's rife among students. As a little girl, I understood that I was getting ready inside, at some level, for a special occasion, and I felt excited. I heard people saying, 'She loves an audience.' And I knew that I loved an audience, and that I responded to an audience. In spite of actually being quite a shy little girl, there was something that emanated from the audience that I could use and I did use it. And of course, the audience loved it—I mean, the younger I was the more they loved it. (It's so harmful the way people dote on the very young. It's very bad for them.) Then I could *use* that excitement. The time before you play is usually very uncomfortable because the excitement is already bubbling, but it's not yet time for action. Once you're in action you can use it, and it falls into place. I think I had understood that from very early on. And so when the chemistry became plain through our anatomy and physiology lessons in Alexander teacher training, of course, that was only a sort of translation into words of what I already knew. And it's not just a matter of 'conquering your nerves,' as they say. That's an unhelpful idea. It implies civil war. But with encouragement and increasing experience one probably does get better at coping, at handling the whole.

I remember in one season when I had a lot of concerts, I started each one with a certain Boccherini sonata. In all, I played that piece twenty-three or twenty-four times in the season. And since the season is really only the winter months, that amounts to a lot of performances close together. By the end of the season I could play that piece, as somebody said, standing on my head. I could play it *well* standing on my head. And having played it so often, I had no nervousness about it. But when the situation became a little more difficult, or if I had to play something I didn't know frightfully well, which, of course, often happened, because I had been doing a lot of concerts and often had to fish something out that I hadn't had time to work at as much as I'd have liked to—then I suffered a great deal from nervousness. My experience of being nervous—that's to say, when the excitement doesn't get liberated into the

---

[1] ' . . . can you imagine that I have not known any artist as tormented as I am with nerves? The thought of a public concert always gives me a nightmare . . . even now.' *Conversations With Casals*, p. 200.

playing—was like being completely enclosed in a plastic membrane which was just a little too small that I needed to get out of and couldn't.

JA. Yes.

VM. And I'd sometimes have a sensation of my fingers turning inside out and running away up inside my arm, running into hiding, so I was left there with nothing in my fingers. And that of course is all because of 'pulling down' and shrinking and all the fear stuff that we now understand through the Alexander Technique.

JA. You saw the nature of it more and more clearly as you had Alexander lessons?

VM. Oh yes, oh yes. There was nothing I could do about the nervousness before I had lessons. The sensation was as clear as if I was wrapped in something I couldn't get out of. Only quite transparent, see-through, and it would be like a glass partition between me and the audience.

JA. Maybe you were better at identifying it than others because Casals had made you so sensitive to the basic requirements of playing, like the elasticity, the percussion, etc., so that it was actually the 'fingers' you acquired with Casals that were running up your arm and hiding, rather than your common everyday ones you had before studying with him.

VM. Oh gracious, yes. I like that idea! When I was in Prades, I played to one or two people without any qualms. I thought 'nerves' were at an end! When I came back to England, I thought *all* my troubles were at an end. I had mastery, but I didn't think this with a great deal of conceit. I just thought, "Now all that's out of the way. I can start to work and develop from here and do whatever comes next.' Cover the ground. Make a career. Also, I thought I was never going to have to play out of tune again, 'Isn't that a blessing.' Ha! And for quite a long time I really did have the refined intonation I'd acquired in Prades at my beck and call. But through lack of discipline, it tended to get ragged sometimes. And then, of course, as you know, on top of that I had a lot of trouble with my wonderful old cello, which is incidental, though I'm inclined to forget about it; but that was another hurdle.

XXII

BACK TO NATURALLY

JA. But isn't it a fact that, even though you haven't been playing quite as much in recent years, dealing more and more with these basic things within yourself that Alexander allows you to do, has brought you somehow back to where you were when you left Casals?

VM. Yes. Without a doubt.

JA. And that otherwise you would have expected it only could have been done through hours and hours of practice on the cello?

VM. Probably.

JA. So it's important to say that dealing with your use of yourself in daily life—while doing the dishes, while gardening, while giving Alexander lessons, etc—you're always working at improving and maintaining the use of yourself as a whole. And when you work on yourself a lot in this everyday way it tends to foster a constant general growth and development that helps you in many ways to be at the level you were when you left Casals.

VM. Mmm.

JA. So that in spite of the fact that you haven't performed as much in recent years, you're still maintaining many of the elements you need for cello performance just by leading your daily life with a better use of your self.

VM. Yes, you're right. And there is still clarification going on, in a quiet way, of everything I got from Casals. And I'm very surprised to find that people who've heard me over the years say that I play better now than when they heard me earlier. Through sheer passage of time, and better 'use' I suppose.

JA. I certainly find the same thing happens for me on flute even though I'm not playing as much these days.

VM. Yes, I can hear it.
I still don't like to be hurried, though. For instance the chamber music concert that we recently did with Melinda Crane on only three rehears-als—in the trio,[1] I felt I was nowhere near knowing the music as well as I would have liked. This is where I'm not a quick learner. I don't have the orchestral player's skill of playing music I don't intimately know as if I did. You know, I need to *know*, because this skill hasn't been part of my musical experience. And yet the trio went very well and comfortably. Another thing that it took me a long time to recognise is that with Casals there was plenty of time to allow things to mature and develop and take root and that kind of thing, and that I was not developing the skill, which alas is necessary for 'survival in the profession,' of trotting something out with next to no rehearsal.

JA. But even with the Schumann *Fantasy Pieces* you played on that con-cert, though you didn't know Melinda, the pianist, well and didn't have very much rehearsal time with her on them, they came off beautifully.

---

[1] Bohuslav Martinu trio for flute, cello, and piano. Performed by Vivien Mackie, Joe Armstrong, and Melinda Crane in 1984.

VM. What was interesting was that communication between us was so easy. I felt the two of us truly played Schumann as I understand Schumann.

JA. Yes.

VM. I had very, very little to say to her in rehearsal. She did everything I wanted—perhaps because I was clear, as well.

JA. And do you think the factor of your years of Alexander experience tied in there?

VM. I don't know how much that's Alexander experience or how much that's just plain experience. I'd learned the Schumann pieces quite recently, about four years before. So, you can say that I learned those on a background of lots of Alexander experience, and perhaps the way I learned them had something to do with the way it was easy to play the other night. But the Spanish group that I also played included one piece, *Granadina*, that I'd learned a long time ago and played a great deal over the last forty years. It was very exciting that *Granadina* was the one that came closer than anything else that night to the experience I haven't very often had until recently of playing like a child again. Sometimes I think, 'This is how it used to feel.' So that I'm getting back to the time before the dreadful doubt about, 'How do you do this?' when it used to just happen 'naturally.' You remember that in my first lesson with Casals he said, 'Just play naturally,' and that I had realised with appalling force that I could no longer play naturally, and I buried that realisation at once? That idea that I had lost 'naturally' stayed hidden until I had my first Alexander lesson when it popped up again. I thought, 'Ha!—This is how we get back to 'naturally!' And now, on occasion, I feel 'I've got there.' It took Casals, and the Alexander Technique, and the passage of time, to get me back to it. *Granadina* was so exciting. You just throw everything you ever knew away, and it comes back to you. But you can only throw it away if you really deep down know it.

JA. Yes, yes.

XXIII

DEEPER INTO CASALS' TEACHING

JA. Could we go on now to talk more in depth about Casals' teaching and attitude toward music?

VM. Yes.

JA. Did Casals speak in French to you in lessons?

VM. No, he spoke in English, and he always called me 'Miss Couling.' His English was perfectly adequate for the teaching, but sometimes it was a little bit quaint. As when he said, 'from up! Play this note from up!' That was good and graphic. Quaint as it was, I don't think he could have expressed that better. Now that I know about the Alexander Technique, hindsight tells me *how* good that idea was. Especially as he demonstrated it perfectly.

JA. Can you describe how he did it?

VM. Well, this particular time that I'm remembering he demonstrated—because it was always better than trying to explain—and he swooped his bow down and gathered up the note, like a hawk swooping down from the sky to gather up a rabbit.

If I asked him a question he would quite often be foxed. But then I hardly ever did ask questions, because I found that as soon as I had framed a question in my mind I found I knew the answer already. The same with the Alexander Technique; in the Alexander learning, when I'd composed my question, I found that if the answer was not at my fingertips, then it was potentially there in my understanding, if I only waited for it. And this suggests something to me about all good teaching. When you ask a question, the answer is inherent in what you've learned already. What you've already learned contains the potential of what you're going to learn next, and so on. So this is why I didn't ask Casals many questions. And a good example of this is when we came to the end of the first year, as I think I've already said, I suddenly remembered I'd been told I must ask him about my vibrato. 'Vivien, for Heaven's sake get Casals to do something about your vibrato while you're over there!' So I asked. And he said, 'Vibrato? But you have a beautiful vibrato.' And I realised he was right! So the answer to the vibrato problem I had had was in the way the finger made contact with the string, and how my arm behaved in consequence. The offending vibrato cured itself of its own accord, which was amazing. So it seems to follow that special vibrato exercises on top of an inadequate, improper, unreasonable means of making contact with the string are a waste of time.

JA. Yes! That makes me think of that time during our Alexander Training when we decided to experiment and see if I could produce a vibrato for you while you were merely bowing a long, straight sound and you let me create the undulation with the palm of my hand just from a gentle contact in the middle of your back, quite low below your shoulderblades—and it worked beautifully!—because you were going up so well in the whole of yourself and were keeping a good contact with your finger on the string. And it was all the more amazing because there was very little visible movement going on in your finger, hand, wrist, or arm—especially in comparison to the extreme waggling you see so many other string players doing to produce their vibrato.

VM. Oh, yes, I remember that!

What was extraordinary was that while I was learning with Casals just to be accurate and to put the right finger down in the right way in the right place at the right time, and all the things that the work at this early stage entailed, I was doing something very fundamental to *me*—it got right to my soul. The precision in taking the notes 'off the page' and making them audible.

JA. The muscular action of it?

VM. Yes, and the mental accuracy too, because they're essentially the same thing. The greater the accuracy is, the finer the point of the tool becomes and the deeper it cuts, the deeper it engraves. It draws lines on your deepest experience, and scratches, etches, at that level so that, in a way, your deepest experience is brought to the surface, to the light, and illumined. So the more clarity you have, the more the pictures come up from greater depths.

JA. And not just at the beginning of a note, but also in getting from one note to the next?

VM. Yes. Both. It's quite a journey within yourself just getting from A to B! It's a job that you're doing, but it just does involve you right down there at your roots, in spite of it's being apparently only a matter of playing the right note at the right time. It just involves so much of you.

JA. A wholer kind of living in oneself?

VM. Yes.

XXIV
CASALS, AND LIFE AND ART

VM. I remember thinking, quite early on, 'My goodness, I'm getting far more than cello lessons here.' And I suppose I thought it was something to do with philosophy in a vague way, but at the time I thought no more about it, and got on with the job.

JA. Yes.

VM. I realized it was quite a complete education, that was. The stirrings at that deep level seemed to gather into a current and carry us along. Until right at the end of the three years, when I was racing through the repertoire in less and less time, I was beginning to draw on the 'capital' I'd accumulated. But at the very beginning, the work was an engraving on my substance, somehow. And of course it is, literally, engraved in your brain. You're creating extremely fine, intricate pathways. They cut deep, don't you think, in some sense?

JA. Yes! So it was as if working in that way on music was also really bringing you in touch with the whole of life itself in a deeper way.

VM. What do you mean?

JA. Well, becoming more in touch with the world in terms of nature and emotion, feeling, etc. From knowing you as long as I have, I suspect that even before going to Prades you were somebody who was always drinking in every little bit of daily life that you saw and felt. But I also suspect that the experience of going into music with Casals and working on it at such a great depth also deepened your capacity to feel and appreciate other things even more in your daily life as well.

VM. Yes, probably.

JA. That it made whatever you were confronted with in life just that much more vivid.

VM. Vivid, real, yes. Intensity is like that, isn't it?

JA. Yes. So you wouldn't just leave your cello lesson and say, 'Well, now that's my lesson. The lesson's over, and now I'll go off and get on with the business of living—shopping, cooking, etc. as if it was totally unaffected by what had happened in the lesson.

VM. No . . . This is why, you see, it doesn't really mean anything to me to talk about 'Art.' You know, I never think, about playing as Art. 'It's *living*!' There's blood in there. This is why I say, you know, there has to be blood in what I do. It has to come from the bones, from down there where it hurts. Or where it may hurt, rather. In among the nerves, as down in the root of a tooth, where it's very very close to the core of you and exquisite agony is just around the corner! And there again you sort of come full circle. It's rather the same as when Dewey refutes the idea that art has to be something that's reserved for the museum. Or the pedestal. And that only the elite are able to go and enjoy it, if they have enough money, and enough education, enough culture to appreciate it.[1]

JA. Yes.

---

[1] John Dewey, *Art as Experience*, Putnam's Sons, New York, 1934, pp. 1-13.

VM. But if a painting or a piece of music really has the 'blood' in it, then everybody should be able to have it as part of their lives, just like the grass and the sky and the sea.

JA. Amen!

VM. Do you remember when we went to see the 'Mise en Tombeau' in the church at Corneilla on the way up Mt. Canigou above Prades when we were there in 1986?

JA. I'll never forget it!

VM. The figures are carved in wood, 18th century or so—though they look quite prehistoric—about three feet tall. There's Mary Magdalene, and Joseph of Arimathea, and others—I forget who they all are—standing round the tomb of Jesus, and those characters are carved in pure sorrow. There's grief in every line, and they are so moving. And in a way, not a bit beautiful. There's a truth and reality about them that transcends mere beauty. And I don't know if they're the work of a known fine artist or some peasant village carver, but they are absolutely profoundly moving things. You know, I used to walk all the way up there to look at them quite regularly. They're in a very dark corner of the church, and you don't see them until you've been in the church for some time and your eyes have become accustomed to the lack of light. I was in there one day and two ladies came in. They didn't see me because I was in an even darker corner. They were looking at the figures, and one said to the other, 'On dit qu'ils bougent.' ('People say they move.') I used to have the feeling that if I put my hand into their alcove among them, I'd put my hand into another world. They really seem to have, these very simple and perhaps not beautiful figures, an extraordinary power about them.

JA. Yes, and *anyone* can sense it immediately.

XXV

CASALS AND EXPRESSION

JA. This might be a place where we could speak of Casals' attitude about beauty of tone and vibrato.

VM. Well, he said right at the beginning that the sound must always be beautiful. But he seemed to me not to be concerned with 'beauty of sound' as I knew it. If I had to describe in words the kind of sound he always made, I would say that he always looked for a 'truth' of sound rather than a beauty—rather as those plain carvings in the church carry so much feeling in their plainness. Casals had a directness, a straightforwardness of sound. A plain utterance, so that you knew exactly what he was saying. And that sometimes unexpectedly resulted in the most stunning beauty.

JA. Yes, that's so characteristic of all his recordings too, in spite of the scratchiness of the old recording techniques; but I think because of that poor fidelity many people don't appreciate that quality of 'plain utterance' because they're listening for what's more fashionable today as beautiful cello sound. And this reminds me of the time when one of the very accomplished cellists in the Alexander string courses we gave together in Boston played a movement from one the Bach suites. She certainly did it very well from a conventional standpoint. But then you asked her to play the 'story' of it to someone you had come and kneel on the floor right in front of her, and she 'told' the Bach right into the girl's eyes. The difference was incredible, and everyone sensed it immediately. And when she finished you said, 'The first time it sounded like a beautiful slab of polished mahogany that you could admire for its colour and grain and sheen but you couldn't see through.' Everyone laughed, including the cellist, because they knew you were right on the nickel—and especially since I think most of the class had initially been quite impressed with the mahogany slab and would have been content to accept that as a very good account of the music.

VM. Yes, I think so too. I almost did myself!

I think one of the things that I thought was so marvelous about Casals' playing was that he did something that I'd never noticed anyone else doing in quite the same way—he *spoke* as well as 'sang' on the cello. 'Beauty of tone' had always seemed to me to suggest singing. I'd always assumed, and all my teachers and everyone around me always assumed, that you wanted a singing tone. 'A singing tone is a beautiful tone, and a beautiful tone is a singing tone.' I'd never heard anyone simply *say* anything on the cello as Casals did. He simply said things, or even mumbled or murmured. And then there would be song. And then there would be colour. He doubled his range of expression straight away by allowing a kind of speech level to come in. He also doubled his range of colour by using 'no-vibrato' in a very positive way. In fact no-vibrato was the starting point, and he brought vibrato in as a special ingredient when it seemed to be necessary. He didn't blanket everything with vibrato at all. In the early days when I was just searching for the notes and we were listening, listening, listening, we didn't use vibrato. And we worked a very great deal without vibrato in scales and exercises. Then it just seemed to come in as required—of course we did use it in the Haydn concerto. I saw what he was doing and I did it. 'No vibrato'? No vibrato, then. So early on I became steeped in the notion that no-vibrato is acceptable. It's one of the expressive possibilities that you have available. It's one of the things that's a legitimate part of the range of sounds on the cello, and sometimes no-vibrato is 'what's necessary.'

JA. Yes, and it might be important to point out here for some readers that there are musicians who play practically nothing without vibrato . . .

VM. Yes—expressiveness and beauty of tone seem to be equated with a constant vibrato.

JA. Usually undulating at a constant speed. And for them it also seems linked up with their idea of playing with fullest expression. Not just string players, but wind players and singers too. And in many cases, it actually seems to me to be limiting them very much, especially if they're producing it in a forced or contrived way.

VM. Yes. One well-known British teacher used to say that sort of vibrato sounds like a nervous disease!

JA. Yes!

XXVI

BLOOD, SWEAT, AND A TEAR OR TWO

VM. That reminds me of one of my first experiences on those Sunday evenings, when I heard Casals' recording of Bach's first gamba sonata. I wasn't familiar with the gamba sonatas at all—in fact I'd never even heard them. We came to the slow movement, and I found it quite, quite breathtaking. It's a simple movement, it's true, but it was such a clear performance from both Casals, and I think, Horszowski on the piano, that when I got home I would have been able to write it down almost in its entirety. I remembered absolutely clearly how it went. This very simple movement culminates in a long, long E for the cello, while the keyboard builds up slow, climbing arpeggios of ever-increasing span against this continuing E. It goes on, and on. And up to that day, I would have taken for granted that if you had a long note like this to play, which has to get louder and louder all the time, then that crescendo must be most perfectly graded and there must be a seamless joining at each change of bow. The changes must be absolutely inaudible—and I would have practised it along those lines.

But what Casals did in this performance was—he put his bow on the string, and it ground quietly along during the first two arpeggios on the keyboard, and then when he got to the end of the bow, he changed direction and began the journey back. The change of bow was clearly perceptible as I recall, and I remember thinking, 'That wasn't a seamless change!' So he went on to the next stage in the growth of that E, and it was really like the growth of something in nature—where the skin splits, and something new appears. All the time there was this tremendous increase of span in the piano arpeggios, trying to split the skin of the cello note, more and more, so we could see more and more of what was under it, and the swelling went on, and the vibrato—(vraayaayaayaayaaya) —became closer and bigger and bigger and BIGGER and the arpeggios were climbing and climbing and climbing, and the span was getting E N O R M O U S, and then all of a sudden that E *burst* open, and out came a sheet of flame or a cry or something. And out of me came tears and sweat. And I thought, '*Well*! That's what Bach was at; he was building up tension! My goodness, yes!' I really had been through something by the time the tension broke. And there would have been no 'bursting' if he had played it with a smooth seamlessness and 'beautiful tone' from moment to moment all the way along, instead of raw, urgent *sound*. But if you took an inch, say, a square inch out of that long cello E—if you can imagine doing such a thing—and you had a look at it up close, it would look like rough crocodile skin, or something like that. And you'd know that there was something *big* in there.

And that was perhaps the strongest musical experience in the smallest compass of time that I have ever had. I was taken to the very edge of emotional containment. The tears that came were momentary tears. I don't mean flowing tears, just one and a great gasp. And since we were listening to the record in Casals' presence, it wasn't the kind of social situation where people were going to chit-chat, or anything like that, about the performance. It wasn't going to be evaluated or criticised; so I was able to have this huge experience all to myself in fact, and go home, as I said, and know the whole movement by heart from start to finish.

JA. Could you say perhaps that the reason the experience was so power-ful was because there was so much meaning in it? That it meant some-thing different in an earthbound, natural way that 'beauty of sound' and 'seamless joinings' couldn't convey?

VM. Oh, absolutely. It was a real glimpse of suffering becoming unbear-able and suddenly being relieved. *That* isn't smooth and seamless.

XXVII

'ORDER, BUT WITH FANTASY'

JA. I ask that as a leading question, you know.

VM. I realise that. I don't need much leading, because I'd like to tell you next . . . Did you have more to say?

JA. Yes, but I'd rather have you go ahead anyway.

VM. Well, I just want to tell you next about a much later experience that was closely related to that one in the Bach. It was in a lesson with the two of us playing the slow movement of the fourth Beethoven sonata. It's very brief, it's hardly a movement at all. It's more of an introduction to the last movement. And in the whole of that introduction, Casals used vibrato on four notes. I counted. Only four notes [—out of 146 as we've just counted them from the score]. Now, I think this short movement has a condensed *Fidelio* in it, or something of the essence of *Fidelio*.[1] Black and dark and confined, and it goes deeper and deeper and deeper into a dungeon. And then there is the sublime moment when a sudden shaft of light appears. Years later I was playing this sonata at a lecture-recital, standing in for a colleague who was ill, with a pianist I'd only just met, and in his talk the pianist said of this moment, 'Here, a heavenly character walks past the window.' And my thought had always been, 'There's an angel, it's an angel!' But there had been absolutely no discussion about the piece between the pianist and myself, and I thought how exciting it was that we saw this movement in the same light—or the same 'dark!' The great, black, descending octaves aren't softened by any vibrato. They're like stone stairs going down into Purgatory, a new depth of grimness at each step. And I thought of Strauss's *Death and Transfiguration*. Strauss' version is quite long. Beethoven does it in four lines. But Casals did it in four-notes-with-vibrato in those four lines. Four vibrating notes. You asked about meaning—well, for me, this little movement conjures up not only the whole of *Fidelio* but Dante's *Inferno*. It's on that kind of scale.

JA. Yes! Would Casals ever say anything very specific like that about the meaning or import of a piece you were working on together?

VM. No, he would just make enormous gestures, or quite often his eyes would fill with tears, and he'd pat his heart with a little gesture and say, 'Oh, so *beautiful*!' or '*Wonderful*!' or '*Oh*!. . .' you know? But nothing about any actual meaning.

JA. I remember a quote somewhere in the *Conversations* with Corredor where Casals is talking about the essential components of music being like the natural rhythms that come from the steps of dance and that come from song, and he also says that he would often ask his students, 'What do you feel, what do you see? An artist has imagination and fantasy and when he gives himself to music he ought to feel and see things, however vague and indefinite the vision.'[2]

---

[1] Beethoven's opera *Fidelio*, first performed in 1805, involves the imprisonment of Florestan, a valiant fighter for freedom, left by Pizarro, his ruthless enemy, to languish and starve with other guiltless fellow prisoners in a foul, dark dungeon. Leonora, Florestan's wife, disguises herself as a youth, Fidelio, and gains entrance to the prison, confronts Pizarro, and frees Florestan and the others from their chains and darkness.

[2] *Conversations with Casals*, p. 158, 194.

VM. I don't remember him ever asking me anything like that. He occasionally gave a little 'nudge,' about the 'legend' feel in the third movement of the Lalo concerto, for instance . . . .

Of course 'rainbows' was one of his trademarks,[3] but I heard that more often in his master classes than in my lessons. He certainly made a great many 'rainbow' gestures though, and the gesture was more eloquent than the word. The word immediately suggests the colours, and it's pretty. The gesture is not intrinsically pretty. It's big and expressive.

. . . Oh yes, and at the very end of the Beethoven G minor Sonata, he would shout, as we got faster and faster towards the final chords, 'Kermesse!' My dictionary defines that as—of all things—'a cycle race held in an urban area!' But I didn't know that then, and I'm not entirely convinced that's what he had in mind; it made me think of a rather wild village fiesta. But hurtling downhill to the finishing line, definitely.

JA. Do you suppose the level you were working on together automatically included a kind of intuitive understanding of the music's meaning? And I mean 'intuitive' in the sense that Susanne Langer [an American philosopher of aesthetics] does when she says, 'The act of intuition whereby we recognize the idea of "felt life" embodied in a good work of art is the same sort of insight that makes language more than a stream of little squeaks or an arabesque of serried inkspots.'[4]

VM. Yes, I do!

JA. So there wasn't really much need for him to interject many verbal analogies or metaphors?

VM. No, Casals never did that with me. Well, I was full of pictures and metaphors anyway, without anything being said to feed them. I had very clear pictures of what goes on in the music like the 'heavenly character walking past the window.' Casals and I hardly, if ever, talked about it.

---

[3] On the recording, *Casals: Musician of the Century* (Columbia Masterworks LP, M5 30069, M30216), which includes segments on Casals conducting and teaching, he says: 'Every phrase is a *rainbow*!' And then he plays several successive phrases from the second minuet of Bach's first cello suite, saying '*rain*bow, *rain*bow, RAINbow!,' as each phrase grows in breadth.

[4] Susanne K. Langer, *Problems of Art*, 'Artistic Perception and "Natural Light,"' Scribner's, New York, 1957, p. 67.

But when he played the third of the Schumann *Pieces in Folk Style* with me, I thought, though I didn't describe it to myself in words then, 'Here is an old grandmother in an old cottage in the Black Forest sitting in a dark place by the fire, telling a story. She's telling it, not singing it, and her voice is an ancient voice, croaky and hoary with experience. She's telling a fairy story, maybe one of the Grimm fairytales. And then this brightly colored picture comes: there's a knight on a white horse, and you see him coming from far off, as in a mediaeval illuminated manuscript, light and bright, enameled green grass, and shining armour. He has a trumpet, too. It's absolutely clear to me—and there is the picture of the princess in the tower. You see her from the knight's point of view. He's down there, coming towards her. The princess is wearing pink, and has a long pointy hat, and she has long, long hair that she's going to let down from the window all the way to the ground, so that he can climb up it. And then the grandmother goes on with the story.' I get all this every time I play the piece, and of course if I hear someone else play it and I don't get all this from their playing, I feel immensely deprived. Once I played this piece with a pianist I hadn't previously met, and he said, 'There's a princess in a tower, isn't there?' I said, 'Yes—and there's the knight.' That was another example of sharing the pictures spontaneously. Schumann must have been steeped in all this German culture and folklore, and when you play his notes, these are the pictures that pop up. (Of course, you could ask: what would I see if I had no experience of these fairytales myself, I wonder? And what would Schumann have said about it himself? That would be interesting to know.) But it's not in any way like making a movie sound track to accompany the action in a story—the very opposite.

JA. Yes. But in Schumann's case I don't think it would be all that far-fetched since he himself claimed to have composed his *Davidsbundler Dances* influenced by the different aspects of his own personality in the forms of 'Florestan' and 'Eusebius.' So I can't think he'd mind your associations and intuitions at all!—especially if they brought the music more to life as you were playing it. But there are probably a lot of poststructuralists who'd have a heart attack if they heard us talking in, what they call, 'such a "crypto-subjective" manner'!

VM. Yes! So Casals never said, 'Imagine here a princess in a tower.' Never anything like that. We played the notes. We played them accurately. We did what was written—and the pictures came. The grandmother has a voice without vibrato, a grandmother's voice. She comes in with the story a couple of times more, and then there's another glimpse of the knight and the princess, and that's the end of the piece. So Casals very seldom spoke of pictures, but sometimes he would make gestures that made it clear that this was to be 'pompous,' or 'very tender,' or 'softer,' or more 'dressed up.'

JA. Yet it seems that even when you began lessons with him and stayed on the first three lines of the Haydn so long there was a sense that each small thing you worked on so meticulously also contained within it the expression of some kind of life experience.

VM. Oh, yes.

XXVIII
'FANTASY, BUT WITH ORDER'

JA. You weren't just working on intonation and articulation and sound only for their own sake, but for the full realisation of the life experience embodied in the notes.

VM. Mmm. And you might even say we never even talked or thought in terms of mere 'technique.' I probably expected that we were going to do some strictly 'technical' work, and even asked him about it, but all he said was "The scales, the scales.' And I got to thinking, 'What is technique? Is technique not acquiring the means to do what you have to do? What you need in order to obey necessity? To do what is necessary?' And working as we were, were we not accomplishing exactly that? The remarkable thing was that after the first grueling year I was expecting to spend the whole second year on the Haydn sonata as Vera had predicted, and yet I found instead that we already had the wherewithal to tackle the Dvorak. And the Dvorak brought with it certain other elements. And then we took all that we had gathered and applied it to the Bach suite, and then we added the Schumann pieces to my repertoire, and then something else, and so on. And as we went along, we took less and less time on the pieces, because more and more the 'means whereby' was available to do what the music required.

JA. But even towards the end of studying with him would he still occasionally take you through a phrase in 'slow motion' so that you could magnify every aspect of it all along the way from beginning to end?

VM. Yes, that was a perennial.

JA. A way of working that could always be used to great value?

VM. Yes. What comes to mind when you ask that question is, more or less, his idea about 'long notes.' In the Haydn for example, I had already learned in the first bar or two that every note, as I said before, is either coming towards you, or going away. It has a direction. It's never just there; and it mustn't go along just plain. The ear demands to be intrigued and fascinated. If you present the ear with a steady, unchanging sound, it quickly loses interest and ceases to pay attention.

JA. It just says, 'O.K. That's *that* sound. Fine. Now what *else* is there?'

VM. Yes. The steady sound recedes into the background of attention, doesn't it, like a burglar alarm or the noise of workmen in the street, after they've been going on for a while? Sometimes a long note is like an egg—what is to come is already developing in there—and that has to be clear to the listener. I remember when a violinist played the Bruch concerto in one of the Alexander string classes we gave here in Boston last year. I felt that the first note of all is a giant egg, and the whole first movement comes out of it. And everybody has to know it's an egg. I mean, the note even *looks* like one on the page!

JA. Yes, it's true!

VM. But you have to *make* it so, and an egg that's full of developing content—and then, out of it the baby bird comes, and it goes on and on developing.

But of course there is the whole big and interesting question here about the organ, which can't significantly change a note once it's begun—and other keyboard instruments which can't sustain a sound!

JA. I guess that's when they have to rely on what they call 'agogics,' or slight rhythmic alterations, to give that sense of growth, etc. So often you see players of those instruments doing so much extraneous movement that it makes you think they must be trying to compensate for that lack of access to the greater flexibility of sound almost all other instruments have.

So this process of Casals blowing something up and looking at it was happening to some degree all the time?

VM. Let's say 'enlarging.' Enlarging was really happening all the time. Oh yes, oh yes.

JA. Might you even say that this was the main activity you were doing?

VM. Well, I felt it was working under a microscope. Yes, that's all we were doing. And when you once prodded me into saying we didn't ever work on the seamless joins, you made me realise that we didn't ever work on that type of 'technique' thing per se.

JA. Yes.

VM. We worked on the music. And if the music demanded seamless joins, of course, seamless joins there had to be. And there were. The *intention* ultimately created the skill.

JA. That's a great way of putting it! It's interesting to think about the microscope analogy, because it often seems to me that the opposite is true with many musicians—that they work through a 'telescope.'

VM. What do you mean?

JA. I mean that the essence of the music seems to get pushed further *away* in their playing because they're trying so hard to get all the notes, fast and brilliant and dazzling and all; but there's very little actually happening in simply getting from one note to the next that has much of any consequence to it expressively.

VM. Yes, well said!

XXIX

GETTING RID OF CLUTTER

VM. I used to think of how I was brought up, as most players are, on studies to develop velocity that went on and on, repeating the same figures in all sorts of keys over a page or two. I hated them, and I wasn't good at them. Those studies are positively designed to induce stiffness, for good physiological reasons; and of course stiffness is the arch-enemy of velocity. I wasn't good at fast things at all. I more or less squeezed by with those. I had made my childhood reputation on my beautiful slow playing.

Looking back on it, I see now that fast stuff was not at all easy for me until I learned at last that I had to get rid of *clutter*. And then, of course, if you've got clear notes with no clutter between, you can put them as close together as you like.

JA. Can you say what you mean by 'clutter?'

VM. Well: questionable intonation, and any shuffling to try to correct it; and inadequate articulation, and any sort of doubt. And of course, looking at things up close so that you can see exactly what you've got and where the music is going will show you exactly where and what the clutter is.

JA. So you're constantly working to get rid of it.

VM. Yes. That's why we spent so much time under the microscope! Everybody knows that slow practice is the way to work at fast passages, but this microscope work was very different from my old idea of 'slow practice!' What's more, we never had a look to see if a passage was ready to go fast yet, or not; there were no 'half-way houses.' When everything was perfectly clean and clear, then it was ready to go fast and testing wasn't even required. One day I played him my slow C# minor scale so well that he asked me to do two, three, even four octaves to a bow. I would never have dreamed of trying four octaves to a bow—that has to be really, *really* fast. But he said, 'The F# on the way down was not right.' And I spotted it too when I 'replayed' it in my memory. *That's* what the slow practice was for. So we didn't do studies for speed—or 'spiccato' or 'sautillé' or 'up-bow slurred staccato'—in fact Casals never even used those words. 'Staccato,' yes, and 'legato;' he would use those. He used all sorts of vocal sounds instead—for instance, 'tuh-*tuh*!' or 'lugga-dugga!' and so on—which showed very clearly what he wanted. With all possible vocal sounds and all the letters of the alphabet at your disposal you have an infinite variety of possibilities for describing, for instance, the beginning of a note—you can start with a vowel, you can start with a 'buh' or 'tuh' or a 'fuh' or a 'whuh.' All those ways, and lots more. An instruction like 'harder attack' or 'gentler attack' is better expressed in sounds like those—there's something to imitate, not something to interpret and guess at. If you limit yourself to the standard 'techniques' that most people learn—even if you develop a very good 'sautillé' or 'spiccato'—you may not gain the flexibility that allows for negotiating musical 'corners,' or for the transition from melody to decoration and back that happens so often in the Dvorak concerto, for instance. What's difficult, and so lovely when it's beautifully managed, is the transition which takes you from one passage into the next. Even within a passage with a pattern that makes it look the same all through on the page—like wallpaper—you still have to be able to mould and model.

XXX

GETTING RID OF
CLUTTER ILLUSTRATED

JA. Yes! The idea of getting rid of 'clutter,' reminds me of the day you took me through 'Do this' in a cello lesson, because I think maybe getting rid of clutter is the main thing it helped me to do—or should I say, forced me to *have* to do. Whether or not you were intending that to be part of the bargain, I'm still not sure.

VM. I'd be interested in hearing your take on it after all these years. And then maybe I'll tell you mine!

JA. Well, we were having a lesson one evening in your music room after you'd invited me over for dinner with you and the boys. But even then,

I don't think we were calling them 'lessons'—merely 'doing some cello.' Anyway, since we had two cellos available (unlike at school where we usually only had the one I was using) you sat down at yours opposite me once I'd got mine out and tuned. And suddenly, you said, 'O.K., Joe, do this.' And you played a big, dramatic, flourishing note—or at least what seemed so to me. It was full of intensity and complete cellistic artistry, as far as I was concerned, and *way* beyond anything I could imagine myself capable of playing at that early stage of learning, even though I guess by then we'd covered most of the basics that would be involved in it.

I was so astonished to think that you'd consider me in any way capable of playing that way, never mind even being able to find the note or making any attempt at the bowing, etc. I was just totally baffled and verging on being quite embarrassed by feeling completely inadequate in every possible way. I was sure that all my insecurities from college ear-training were about to be brought roaring to the surface, and I was one step away from being wholly terrified. I think I just went blank with all this bundle of emotions and consternation. So I had to ask you to play it again.

So you played the same thing again. Just as dramatically as before. I think I somehow found the gumption to protest a little, or to simply say that I didn't see how I could possibly do something so 'accomplished.' But scarcely had I said it when you immediately said, 'do this' and played it again. I somehow had my wits about me enough to realise that you weren't going to take 'no' for an answer—as you usually never did!—so I thought, 'Well, I could at least *watch* to try to see what she is actually doing if I'm even going to begin to try it at all—although I'm sure that I'll fail completely, because I know I just can't do "that sort of thing."' So I think I asked you to show it to me one more time. You played it, and I watched. And I finally saw *something*, at least. I saw that you did a down-bow, and that it was on the G string and that it was with your first finger playing somewhere near the middle of the string, I think. So I just went ahead and tried to do it, still totally convinced that it would be all wrong and you'd think me a total failure as a cello student.

Sure enough, it was 'awful'! Nothing at all, it seemed to me, of what you played—with all your 'mastery,' etc. etc. And then I immediately felt I needed to go into this extreme negative, self-deprecating reaction, chastising myself for being so inadequate as a musician, etc. But while I was putting myself through all this stuff, you simply said again, 'do this,' and you played the note again. Of course, I completely missed seeing and hearing it because of my being involved in my all my reactions and everything. So I very soon realised that kind of thinking and doubt and self-criticism was getting completely in the way of ever even trying to see if I could actually learn something from the process.

You, though, seemed confident that I could, and that must have been a big help to me, because I was sure ready to pack it in right then and there and go home very embarrassed and convinced that it would take me another ten years to get anywhere nearly so good as to be able to do what you were asking me to do. So I made myself watch again, trying this time at least to look and listen more closely. And then I tried it again. It was still 'all wrong' of course, but somehow I suddenly realised that I could *use* that 'wrong attempt' to get information for listening more carefully to hear what I needed to know in order to try to see if I could get at least a little closer to what you were doing—in pitch, if nothing else. And I think that in one or two more attempts I actually got the note—which, in itself, was a source of utter amazement to me. But you kept on. I finally started to be able to observe more of your gesture, the sweep of the bow, and the kind of attack, etc. And I actually started to get pretty close to what you were doing fairly soon afterward. Total incredulity! About that time, James and Andrew, who'd been playing some game on the floor under the piano, seemingly oblivious to what we were doing, poked their heads out and said, 'Mum! He got it!' And then they started getting intrigued in the whole 'game' of it too.

But you still didn't stop there, you immediately said again, 'Do this,' and you played several *more* notes added on to the first. Again, 'total impossibility' washed all over me. But since I realised that I had to at least chuck all that out and just watch you, I did—even though the same inner struggle and castigation was still lurking in the background of my thinking. But then we seemed to be able to progress much more quickly, and you kept adding bit by bit until, before long, I realised that you actually had been secretly teaching me the 'Prelude' from Bach's third cello suite! And in a little while you had taught me the *whole first phrase*, and I was playing it 'full out'—as a dancer/choreographer pupil of mine used to say when she was performing or practising with no reservations or restrictions whatever. I was actually playing part of a Bach cello suite—*on the cello!*—something I couldn't even have dreamed possible for another ten years, if ever. And I was playing it 'for real' too—not just an awkward schoolboy's scramble for the notes. Everything was all there musically. I think it was about the most gratifying and astonishing learning experience I've ever had—on many, many levels. Not only was it a musical triumph, but it was an enormous personal triumph over all my inner demons and doubts. So I guess what this means in the context of our discussion on 'clutter' was that I was really learning to inhibit my clutter on the most profound level.

And I'm not sure that I could have done it if I hadn't had so much Alexander experience under my belt by then either. I had learned to inhibit unwanted responses in many other aspects of living, so this was an extension of it that I realised I needed to take responsibility for *immediately* if I was going to learn anything at all from you then. And I know this might strike a lot of people as simply being my own particular attitudes or foibles at issue, but over the nearly thirty years or so since then that I've taught the Alexander Technique to many professional musicians, I've seen over and over the same kind of reaction patterns in them to making a mistake or not performing in the way they think they should be able to when they play in front of me in a lesson—even on the instrument they've studied for years and years and on pieces that they are very familiar with. They still put in all that clutter of self-doubt and self-criticism, and it very much blocks them from learning a better way of listening and working through the Alexander point of view. What do you think?

VM. Well, I think all that is splendid stuff. I had no idea you were going through all that! That's your recollection of the event, and what you've learned from it. Now let me tell you the story from my end.

The whole point of the 'Do this' game—and I learned it from Casals—is that the pupil only gets one chance to take in what he has to give back, and it has to be done *at once*. I remember even now the first note I played you, and how I played it. When you say you were astonished that I could consider you capable of playing like that, I must say I had a touch of doubt myself. But I didn't let you see that. You protested and said, 'I can't play that!' and I said, 'I don't see why not! You heard it. You saw it. So do it.' I was reluctant to play it again but I did, and you promptly played it back, just right, complete with the accent at the beginning and the huge crescendo. Then I offered you another note, somewhere else on the cello, and you gave me that back, spot on. I got bolder, and gave you a string-crossing, and two or three notes one after the other quite fast—certainly things far beyond what you might have been expected to be capable of for a year or more to come. You gave me them all back at once, spot-on. I was amazed. At last I chose a single, very high note, right at the far end of the fingerboard, about a 'fourth-year note,' and you played it back at once, exactly. That's actually when the boys came out from under the piano. Goodness, were you really suffering that much? I think you've blown that all up in your mind since. So I think your emotional turmoil, doubt, and so forth must have been running at such a rate that you just *imagined* I'd played that first note quite a number of times. I'd have abandoned the game rather than do that. It would have been *pointless*. As it was, I was thrilled and astonished. You seemed to have a burning clarity of perception coupled with the motor ability to reproduce what you'd perceived that cut right through any protestations or doubts within yourself. I think all that emotional ragbag has ballooned up out of all proportion as you remember it—anyway, all that indulgence was simply 'not necessary.' I also remember we tried this game again about three weeks later, but it didn't work. You knew too much by then, and you were trying too hard to see and hear and work out what I was doing, and the shining clarity and innocence had gone. Once I'd seen that ability you had to take in and reflect my offerings so dazzlingly, I saw that *everyone* must have this, underneath the clutter, and my job would be to find out how to teach the cello from now on without destroying that exquisite mechanism.

We did play that other game, when I fed you bits of the C major prelude and you put them together and recognised what you'd been doing, but that was much later. I didn't know it was such a gratifying and astonishing experience for you—I'm delighted that it was!

JA. I'm sure your memory of those times is more accurate than mine since you were the one who actually decided what you wanted to try with me and when. But over the many years since then, do you think you've discovered any more about how to teach and preserve that capacity in someone?

VM. I really don't know. I knew it would be a life-time's job, and I'm not sure I'm any closer, but an amazing experience like that must have left a trace that would always have an influence on my teaching ideas, as I put them into practice. But of course I've been doing very little of that beginner-stage teaching.

JA. But even so, don't you think that all these years of combined Alexander and cello teaching might have given you more ability to contend with the beginner's situation in a way that would help preserve that 'exquisite mechanism'?

VM. Well, I hope so. Those years have certainly led me into quite different ways of regarding the player/cello relationship, so the build-up of clutter should be less. I wouldn't hope to move systematically towards the 'preservation of the exquisite mechanism'—that might take a miracle. And 'systematically *anything*' would tend to preclude the now-and-then flickers of insight that might leave one open to miracle.

XXXI

BACH

JA. So in the beginning of the second year you worked on the Haydn sonata, and then you did the Dvorak concerto in six weeks. And then I thought you said you went on to the Bach fifth suite?

VM. Yes.

JA. But you also said that before you went to Casals you'd thought, 'I mustn't let him get at my Bach!'—so I assume that you didn't put up any resistance when it came to working on the fifth suite, because by then you realised he might have a thing or two to offer your Bach. Can you say more about how you came around to that more receptive place?

VM. Well! It really wasn't at *all* difficult! I think that as soon as I'd heard him in the flesh and I'd heard this 'earth in the blood,' and this huge *reality* about everything he did, then the Bach fell into place—the Bach that I'd heard on those early recordings suddenly made sense. So there was *no* problem about *that*.

JA. There wasn't even the slightest hesitancy.

VM. Oh, *good* heavens, no! No! No. In fact, you see, the moment he said, 'You don't know what you're doing,' and I realised he was right—well, all that about my having anything of my own to offer in the Bach had crumbled—with the rest of the tottering edifice he swept away when he said 'You don't know what you're doing.'

JA. So you were prepared to accept anything that came along?

VM. Yes! Of course I was!

JA. So you got into the fifth suite—and I'm taking for granted that the way you'd already been working came into play there as well—but could you say anything about when it finally did come to working on Bach, where that might have taken you with Bach—that you perhaps hadn't been before?

VM. Well, I think that both from my college cello professor Ivor James and from Olive Woodington, my earlier teacher, I had had some very good ideas about Bach. They both loved the suites. Of course they did. But they didn't regard them—as *nobody* did in those days—as baroque music, to be treated in a 'period' fashion. Nothing like that. So I remember doing the D minor allemande when I was at boarding school, and that already struck me as a great big, grand, organ-like piece. And in college I did two or three of the suites in the kind of rapid, superficial way we had worked there, because there wasn't *time*— to 'take the time it takes.'

JA. Did you play them on recitals?

VM. No, no. I never played Bach in public—that I remember—before I studied with Casals.

JA. So you just prepared the suites for your college cello lessons?

VM. Yes. Yes, you learned them. The stuff we learned in college wasn't all—I'm glad to say—in order to play in a concert.

JA. It was just part of the normal repertoire you studied.

VM. Yes. Stuff you *have* to know—you need to learn. So I didn't have ideas of Bach that needed to be dismantled, really. I mean, when Casals played it it was just like the *tide* coming in. It just *washed* away anything that'd been there before. It was as if the 'old' Bach had been a photograph, and here he was, in person, living and breathing before me.

JA. Can you say more about how that happened?

VM. Well, having it going on in the room with me . . . you see, Casals was the person who played with me, and he played *for* me. The other teachers I'd had would demonstrate little *bits* of things—but they wouldn't actually play with me or for me as Casals did . . .

JA. Yes.

VM. . . . and having this going on a mere six feet away was really—well, you know—*surg*ing and *swirl*ing . . . and *oh*! . . . *won*derful! And I *took* to it! I didn't know the fifth suite at all before I learned it with Casals. I might not even have heard it.

JA. So when you started working on it with him—even right at the beginning, in the prelude—did it seem like you were entering into a different dimension with Bach right then?

VM. With Bach, yes. But this was the dimension that we'd sort of 'measured out' with the Dvorak.

JA. So that by then you were just at a deeper place with music in general.

VM. Yes! Yes.

JA. And you didn't find then, because of *that,* that his Bach was 'exaggerated'—as some people say—or 'too romantic'?

VM. No. The word 'romantic' wouldn't have entered my head. It seemed to me such 'functional' Bach. I wouldn't say you could *dance* to it, exactly. But it, in itself, is—is *dance* . . . and *weight* . . . and animal *movement* . . . and urgent *expression*. It doesn't seem to me to have anything to do with 'romanticness' as I think of it.

JA. Yes. But a lot of the people you hear criticising the way Casals plays Bach—the suites in particular—sometimes say he had such 'strange interpretations' of Bach and that he really went overboard in them.

VM. Well, I haven't heard much of that kind of comment, really. Perhaps I haven't talked about it to many people. I've been surprised to hear a few people imply that they're not totally convinced that Casals' 'interpretation' of the suites is what Bach had in mind when he wrote them.

You know how Casals found the suites in a secondhand music shop and learned them—he was the first person to play them in their entirety—at least *each one* in its entirety. Well, sometimes I wonder if Bach didn't actually have to wait until Casals played the suites to hear what he'd written in them—that if those suites had not lain dormant and waiting to be played for all those couple of hundred *years* . . .

JA. He was the first one to bring them to light.

VM. Yes. And I think they might have been bigger than even Bach realised.

JA. Yes! Well, how would you compare 'your Bach' that you came to Prades with to what you encountered in studying with Casals and hearing him play the suites in person?

VM. Measly!

JA. Ha, ha!

VM. But not intrinsically very different, because, as I said, Olive Woodington and Ivor James—and my mother, who'd taught me piano—had given me some very clear ideas about Bach. I liked their ideas. I think they were basically the same as Casals'.

JA. So the main thing then was that once you started working on the suite with him, you went into it working basically as you *had* been on everything else?

VM. Yes. Except that—by then—I would spend a lesson, say, taking down the fingerings and writing them in on the page so that I could go away and work on it for the next lesson. I wasn't any longer having to 'catch' the fingerings and bowings as they flew by and remember them by listening and watching. And besides, I'd heard Casals play some of the suites 'live'—because along-side the Sunday evenings, there were a handful of occasions when he played in the town, and we could go and hear him. And I remember once he played some of the suites in one of the cafes, upstairs.

JA. Oh, he did?

VM. Yes. Just for some whim, or some occasion. Nothing formal.

JA. When would that have been—in your first year?

VM. No, I think it must have been early in the second year. It was the dead of winter, and I remember his spike was slipping terribly on the marble floor, and one of the students came and put his foot in front of the spike and *held* it there all through the suite!

JA. Ha, ha!

VM. So I'd heard him play them, and they were becoming much more familiar. And, again, by the time we got on to the fifth suite we were carving our way pretty swiftly through the music—so we didn't have many lessons on it.

JA. Yes.

VM. But I had one of the lessons in public—that's to say, one of his former students heard me practising the suite when he was walking along the street and he came and said, 'Could we have a joint lesson on that suite, because I've never learned this one?' So I assumed, naturally enough I think, that he would pay half the fee and that we would somehow share the lesson as well as the cost. But what happened was that this cellist brought along two of his pupils. And Casals felt that wasn't very proper, and he asked my permission. He said, 'Do you mind if these pupils stay?' And I felt, 'Well, I can't very well say, "Yes." So I think I have to say, "Of course not."' And it turned out that I got the whole lesson and Casals was very—well—'generous' with me; and he let me play the whole thing, and he had very few adverse comments to make. That was a novel and exciting experience.

JA. And so by that time, because of what you'd gained already, it wasn't anything like the feeling you'd had the first year at the luthier's when your colleague asked if you'd like to play the slow movement of the Haydn on one of the cellos there?

VM. Absolutely not! No—this special all-playing lesson, really, gave me a bit of a fillip; and it was because of this unusual situation that I found how ready I was to play the movements all through without being stopped.

JA. And also that he didn't mind having you heard by other people as a student.

VM. He would never have thought of that, I'm sure. Just as I would never have thought of trying to please him, he would never have thought of anything but, 'This is the work that we've done, and if you're there listening, that's what you hear.' I don't think he had any pride in his pupils—or desire to show them off. I never thought of that before—I mean, I don't think he was wanting to gain glory from his good pupils!

JA. No.

VM. He wasn't looking for that.

JA. It doesn't seem like his basic attitude and reverence for music would have allowed him to do that anyway. But if it had been in the first six weeks and you were just working from note to note . . .

VM. He wouldn't have allowed anybody to listen. Certainly not. He would have protected me.

JA. But not because he would feel like, 'Oh well, this student hasn't gotten very far, and I don't want somebody listening to him or her . . .'

VM. '. . . to think I'm a bad teacher.'? *No*! 'This person isn't ready to be heard—doesn't want to be heard—in this . . . not-yet-born state.'

JA. Yes. 'It wouldn't be good for him.'

VM. That's right. He was the kindest man. Have I not actually said that? No? Well, he was. And kind enough to tell me the truth, you know. So kind never to gloss over anything or make allowances . . . you know what I mean?

JA. Yes. Then I'm sort of assuming that because you were going on working in the same basic way . . .

VM. Tell me now what you mean by 'the same basic way.'

JA. Well, with such microscopic attention to the details of each phrase—attending to what each phrase requires for its fullest realisation.

VM. By now I think I'd got sort of a built-in microscope, and I was doing that at home.

JA. Yes, that's what I would have thought! And what I want to ask is—assuming he didn't say the kinds of things to you that he says in the recorded master classes like, 'Bach is the God of Music!'. . .

VM. Oh, no. No, no no.

JA. And presumably he would never talk about Bach as if he were giving you a lecture in musicology.

VM. No—he never talked about music when there was music to be played.

JA. But did you have a sense—especially when you were embarking on the Bach—of any special regard in him for Bach?

VM. I think that he was totally devoted to whatever he was playing at the moment. While I was with him, I also learned one or two rather trivial little pieces, and just as when he plays them on his recordings, they are never trivial in his hands. He dignifies everything he touches . . . and enriches . . . and respects every scrap of music—he just loved the sounds. He would often stop and say, 'How beautiful, beautiful!' And just play me two notes with tears in his eyes—'Lovely, lovely!'

JA. So there wasn't a sense that he had more reverence for Bach than anything else you worked on?

VM. No. We weren't treading on sacred ground particularly, no more in Bach than in anything else.

JA. And I suppose that would also be reflected in the sense that he was approaching the suites more as dances, from what you might call his more 'earthbound' Bach.

VM. It seems to me he didn't see things in layers or levels so that it would be earthbound or heavenly—I think he was quite capable of seeing the whole all the time, and it was the earthiness—I don't like the word 'earthbound'—the earthiness of the Bach that made it sublime.

JA. 'Down to earth.'

VM. Yes.

JA. I remember the first time you played for me—it was the allemande from the third suite, and I was so bowled over by the extremes of life and energy you brought out of it—and you happened to make an off-handed comment later that it's a 'wooden shoe dance' . . .

VM. Oh, yes?

JA. . . . and that just hit me over the head like a lead brick!

VM. Like a wooden shoe!

JA. A wooden shoe! . . . because I'd listened to and played (on flute) the suites so many times before—that allemande in particular—but the special 'reverence' for Bach that I'd grown up with all around me and known for so many years would never have let me consider that it could have been about something so 'mundane' as an actual *dance*—that someone might really do.

VM. It didn't allow for wooden shoes.

JA. Let alone in wooden *shoes!* And even though it might have the title 'Allemande,' it was still Bach, and it had to be placed on such a high pedestal that you couldn't possibly allow yourself to find any of those down-to-earth elements in it at all, as if Bach—even his secular music— was always meant for the same reverent attitude that the solemn church-goer would bring to the organ works, cantatas, passions, etc. So it was a real eye-opener for me when you said that; and of course it was all borne out and magnified later by reading Schweitzer[1] and Pirro[2] and thinking about what Casals himself says in the *Conversations* about Bach, like: 'Bach being the universal genius, there is no emotion that has not been expressed by him, except stinginess, meanness and all that is incompatible with a noble mind. In his works you find some feelings which words cannot describe or classify. I have got used to saying that Bach is a volcano.'[3]

---

[1] Albert Schweitzer, *J.S. Bach*, (Breitkopf and Hartel, 1911), Dover, New York, 1966.

[2] André Pirro, *L'esthétique de Jean-Sébastien Bach*, (Librairie Fischbacher, Paris, 1907) Minkoff, Geneva, 1973.

[3] *Conversations with Casals*, Dutton, p. 110.

XXXII

BACH,
ELASTICITY, AND ONWARD

JA. I'd like to try to tie together a lot of what you've just been saying with some of what we covered earlier because I think it might be interesting for people who would like to look more closely at Bach and what Casals realised about all his music, perhaps more fully than anyone, through the cello suites in particular . . . if that's all right with you?

VM. Yes. Of course it is.

JA. Well, as I think I've said before, I hear so many performances of the suites by very fine players that seem to me to be so monochrome in comparison to Casals' recordings of them and the performances I've heard you do of them. I see many of these other cellists trying to throw all kinds of great passion into them, but the results they're getting still don't contain those elements you mentioned of 'dance, weight, animal movement, and urgent expression' in that down to earth way.

And I've often thought that the reason for this huge difference was mainly because these other cellists simply don't have a large enough vision—or the same vision, maybe—that would allow them to see those more 'earthy' aspects in the music, and therefore their 'interpretations' of the suites don't embrace that broader scope.

But from all we've talked about here, it seems so much clearer to me now that the real reason for the difference in performances might really stem from these other players' lack of experience and understanding of the basic elasticity in playing and their lack of ability to use it from moment to moment—along with a true freedom in the bow arm, a willingness to use 'no-vibrato,' and, *maybe especially*, using the kinds of fingerings Casals' discovered—the 'kangaroo capers,' as you called them—that make the fullest use of the elasticity of the left hand, fingers, and arm. And that it's really these 'main ingredients' which—in and of themselves—could reveal to these cellists the far wider range of expressive possibilities in the suites—if only they knew *how* to get in touch with them and use them.

VM. Well, I think that's *absolutely right*. I think so little regard is paid to—or notice taken of—the huge resilience in the cello strings, and in the bow hair—together. I'm thinking this more and more. Of course, now that we have the metal strings, the resilience in the strings is not so marked. But how often I see people driving away, pushing tone in, instead of bouncing it out—as you would on a trampoline! But the bow and the string know how to *play with* each other. And if you can—once you've got your integrity, perhaps through the Alexander Technique—once you've got the engineering of yourself as a whole working *for* you—then you can afford to abandon a lot of what you believe is what you need for making the sounds and for modeling the phrases, because really, you know, with the elasticity in the *instruments* being recognised and used, the phrases seem to model themselves. I've had this experience sometimes when I introduce a bowing to somebody—I did it yesterday,[1] in fact, while I was giving someone a lesson on the Dvorak concerto—I showed her one of Casals' bowings. 'It does *itself*!' she said. 'You can't *stop* it!' That's delightful to hear.

---

[1] January 24, 2000–Boston.

JA. Hm!

VM. So I think there's a huge amount in what you say. And it's not just the elasticity in the player's fingers, as we were talking about at the beginning—concentrating on, focusing on the elasticity in the fingers. As Casals made it clear, it's the whole show! 'Everything is elastic! *Everything!*' I didn't realise so clearly at the time that he meant everything we deal with, although he said so plainly enough.

JA. Yes, it's not just the player.

VM. Yes, not just the player. The cello, the strings, the bow. . . the *earth*! Even the earth, you know, is suspended in space. It's whirling round. It's not attached to anything.

JA. Yes. So as we've implied, all these ingredients can be employed even more fully and effectively with experience in the Alexander Technique, which—among other things—brings about the fullest elasticity of the whole person.

VM. Because the 'structure' is fully there.

JA. Is fully operative.

VM. Is fully operative . . . yes, yes.

JA. So it seems that you might be one of the very few—or maybe even the only one—who possesses *both* the experience of those basic ingredients of cello playing, 'inherited,' as it were, from Casals, and the ability to transmit the understanding and the experience of them—enhanced by your skill in the Alexander Technique.

VM. Well, I'm certainly one of very few who's had that depth of experience of Casals—by that I mean three years—and from the beginning. And very few people now living, if any, have got that. And the Alexander Technique, as I said, threw light on Casals, and Casals threw light on Alexander, and whether or not I have the ability to transmit it is not for me to say. But I certainly do try. And I certainly love trying! . . . and seeing what *happens*.

JA. But your basic ability of knowing how, more and more, to establish the elasticity in the whole person through the Alexander Technique—

along with your understanding of the elastic operations of the hand and arm that make cellists more *available to* the effect of the fingerings and bowings—possibly combines into something even greater to offer than one or the other alone.

VM. Mmm. Of course the great thing about the elasticity is that you have to *let go* into the elasticity. And it's the elasticity that gives you security. And 'letting go into security' is a very strange idea . . . for most players!

JA. Yes! But you also have the ability to see—especially through your training and years of experience as an Alexander teacher—if somebody's able to do that or not.

VM. I think so, yes.

JA. As well as the ability to help them towards it.

VM. Yes. I hope so!

JA. We've also discussed the fact that you've also saved your notations of Casals' fingerings for the cello suites and the idea that you might consider giving a special course for just cellists on the suites, where they could be gone into in the fuller depth that Casals' approach and understanding of them contains—and in a way that couldn't really be conveyed through a printed edition that merely notated his fingerings and bowings. Have you had any more thoughts about that possibility?

VM. Yes! Lots more thoughts. And it's absolutely true that the fingerings and bowings, in and of themselves—as was pointed out to me about forty years ago—are not enough, because they presuppose the existence of this attitude to—or an acceptance of—the elasticity in everything. They aren't compatible with the conception of fingers as 'strong little hammers.' And I've been meeting 'strong little hammers' this very week[2] . . . and having just to throw them out. Throw them out!

JA. Even in the new millennium they're still here!

VM. Yes! But it's sometimes interesting, when people see how well they do without the little hammers, how *ready* they are to throw it all away.

---

[2] January, 2000.

JA. Do you think that in a course that would be full-time for a week, or even two weeks—or even a month, because I don't know how long it would take to go through all the suites in this deeper way. Do you think something really valuable could be transmitted and experienced in a fairly concentrated span of time like that?

VM. Well, I would hope so—for someone who wanted to come and have a real look at all this. Yes. And I think you wouldn't need to go through the six suites in detail, because you'd get the principles and the ideas first in working on a number of movements, and if you were given the fingerings on that basis, you'd know how to *use* them. I'd hate to have to demonstrate them all. Every last one of them!

JA. Yes!

VM. I used to think that seventy years and the six Bach suites would be all you would need for a full and happy life. And of course I shan't have spent my seventy years—at least not my first seventy years—in an exclusive study of the Bach suites. Because, of course, I realise that wouldn't work. You have to bring real living to music making. My teacher Olive Woodington said once, 'My dear, you have no *idea* what a lot of ordinary living you need in order to nourish one performance!' And I thought, 'Mmm! That's one of the best things that's ever been said!' So, if I could have another seventy years for the Bach suites . . . well then I might begin to really get to know them. But I *have* begun. I have begun.

JA. Yes.

VM. But of course they do gestate away quietly, and get permeations from your ordinary life and from the other music you play and sing and hear. And certainly they seem to be the central item in my idea of cello repertoire—what the cello is *for*.

JA. Yes. I was also going to make another point about how, as someone interested in classical music as a whole—even though I'm a flutist—I think the suites form one of the main cornerstones—certainly for understanding and experiencing Bach, but maybe for all music after him, as well. They're not just another group of works—among many, but there's something essential or fundamental in them in what they express about life—in combination, I think, with the cantatas and the passions, where, as Schweitzer and Pirro showed in their books by looking very closely at the expressive elements of the texts together with the corresponding motifs and rhythms of the music, you can see clearly Bach's way of portraying emotion and life—feeling.

VM. Exactly, they've got the texts as well, and so he was stretched into that corner by the necessity of setting the texts to music, perhaps.

JA. Yes. And just because the texts in his sacred works demand the expression of emotions, actions, and the myriad other aspects of life experience involved in them, doesn't mean that the secular works don't embody the same, or maybe even greater, depth of experience too—as we've already pointed out that Casals realised so fully about the suites.

VM. Yes. But I was just thinking, as you were saying that, that one of the great things about the cello suites is that I think they're very accessible to the listener. And one of the things that I want to do—and I hope to do it in my *first* seventy years—is actually work my way through all the solo violin sonatas and partitas—on the violin, held as a cello. Not, of course, to attempt to play them, but just to see what is there. Because I don't find the works for solo violin nearly so accessible as the cello ones.

JA. Yes.

VM. So I think the cello suites have this unique accessibility. And then, Bach wasn't writing them for 'next Sunday.' Or for the Church. He was writing them for his own pleasure, wasn't he? I think.

JA. He must have, yes. Schweitzer, for instance, doesn't say anything about them being commissioned or composed for any specific person or occasion.

VM. So they had to be born, but they didn't have to be born for a purpose.

JA. Yes, yes. So he could give vent in them to his fullest fantasy—his fullest life experience.

VM. Mmm.

JA. And there's the idea that the cello suites, if understood more completely in terms of Casals' approach to elasticity, etc., could then shed light on the violin sonatas and partitas too.

VM. Well I would hope so. I'm going to need all the help I can get to make my way through them.

154

JA. But especially if you were going to play the violin on your knee like a cello, it seems like it would mean that you'd still be approaching them basically through your cellist's elasticity and choosing the fingerings and bowings that would serve the sonatas and partitas in the same way that Casals discovered would best serve the suites, wouldn't you?

VM. Well, I don't know that I'd get so far as to find anything out about violin fingering. The 'kangaroo capers' wouldn't work—the instrument's too small. But now that I've learned to use my fingers the way I do, I wouldn't be able to use them in any other way. So, you know, it will be painstaking, and I won't be trying to do it well. I'll simply be trying to find out what's there. I could listen to umpteen records. I could go to concerts and hear the best players.

JA. You could play through them on the piano.

VM. Yes, I could even do that, and I could read them and sing them in my head, but it wouldn't be the same. The thing is that I'd need to get my flesh and blood rippling with them.

JA. And that can happen best for you because it's *on the strings*.

VM. On the strings. Yes. That's right.

JA. Well, it seems like you've got a lot of work cut out for you!
  Couldn't we say then that the elasticity that Casals brought to cello playing is just as important on other instruments—especially the other strings? But that maybe it's also harder to get at on the upper strings because their smaller size demands that movements of the arms, hands, and fingers be more confined? And that, in a way, the size of the cello seems to have been ideal for exploring and uncovering what elasticity is really about?

VM. Yes. I think that may be one of the respects in which the cello is considered to be 'easier' than the violin or the viola—and you don't have to hold it up to play it, either. Though of course the violin bow is even longer than the cello bow, so right-arm movement isn't at all confined.
  But if you have to sit to play, new difficulties present themselves, even if you have a decent chair, which you often don't get in a rehearsal or concert hall—legs very easily get fixed, for instance, and it's important that they don't. You can see how orchestral players—and chamber music players—keep trying to find a comfortable arrangement for their legs. If the feet aren't just about under the knees, balance can't be good, and

legs will lose their springiness through being tied in a knot under the chair, or spread-eagled and collapsed. Both these states of the legs are ruinous to the integrity of the back. The important thing about elasticity is that it's *there* in all the joints, and in the flesh of the fingertips themselves.

And you're not necessarily freer because you make bigger movements. You can be absolutely *teeming* with minute movement, though it's hardly obvious on the surface. Unnecessarily big movements may be a sign that movement is blocked in the hips and torso for instance. In fact, the very bigness of the double bass can engender all sorts of fixings as you clamber round it. I loved the way Klaus Stoll of the Berlin Philharmonic treated his bass as a pal, standing there beside it till his moment came, when he would reach right down to play all his fabulous high virtuoso stuff, right down there by the bridge, and when it was over, he'd just bounce back to his lovely full height and breadth.

JA. Aha!

VM. Then I think some pianists, especially when they're faced with a grand piano and some big grand piece of piano music, feel they have to do battle with a great inanimate monster. In fact, piano keys will bounce the fingers back up as soon as they get the chance, so there's a beautiful elastic interchange right there at the point of contact. And those hammers and strings inside are playing the same game. The very same day, the very same piano would sound quite different at the hands of Horszowski or Rudolf Serkin. I remember watching Clara Haskil and thinking her hands looked as though they had been moulded by the music of Mozart. Right there at the keys and fingertips the music flowed to and fro, shaping and sculpting as it went, so sensitive was the attention and the contact. You hardly knew whether she was making the Mozart, or it was making her.

And then wind players have the advantage of *having* to breathe. That's good! Ribs have to move when you breathe—though there may be enormous scope for still freer rib movement in all of us, wind players included. Many of us who don't *have* to breathe to play sacrifice breathing in the interest of what we believe to be 'control.' Or then again, woodwind and brass players often seem to be afraid to abandon their embouchure even for a moment, so the lips and mouth muscles can become very set and fixed. But, given elastic conditions, the embouchure can always re-assemble itself in the twinkling of an eye. It just takes courage to let go of it in the first place. And I think it would be true to say that all instruments vibrate the player—just as the player makes the instrument vibrate—as far as the player's elasticity will allow. *Elastic conditions* are what we need, through and through.

JA. Amen! That's certainly the main thing that I feel I took away from my experience of studying cello with you so that I would have the best model for understanding what I needed on flute—even though I had to find it ultimately through very different areas of awareness and control. So my main model for flute playing really became the elastic string playing of Casals, rather than any other flute playing I heard—except for that of my first teacher, Carl Petkoff, who I believe exemplified it too.

VM. Yes. And another thing I'd like to say is, that I tell people nowadays that they should regard practising as a *treat*. As if you've saved up for it. You mustn't drudge your way through it. You do it as an exquisite pleasure. And you surely don't stiffen when you're enjoying a treat!

JA. So if you did the course on the Bach suites, it'd also be done in the context of that 'exquisite pleasure'?

VM. Well, yes, I'd hope so! But what I mean about the 'exquisite pleasure' is—when we remember this business about your whole self being used in the music—that when you get that exquisite pleasure, it has that lifting effect, for instance, that your success in the 'Do this' game did. And the sheer kinaesthetic *thrill*, which you so surprisingly and amazingly mentioned—*that* heightens your perception, and at the same time heightens your capacity to do things, doesn't it?

JA. Yes!

VM. You've got to work from that *extreme*—and not from a dull center where you drudge away and hope to expand outwards. You get to heaven as soon as you can!

JA. Yes! Ha, ha!

VM. If you can give yourself *two notes* that make you think, 'Ah! *Yes!*' *Then* you've changed your whole outlook and your whole . . .

JA. . . . being.

VM. . . . your whole being. Your whole canvas, as it were, or your whole palette. Your sphere of awareness.

JA. So that each time you come to your instrument, it really needs to be basically a great adventure.

VM. Absolutely! And you need to treat your instrument with the greatest respect—because it is a 'live' thing.

JA. And the great excitement and delight comes because it's an adventure.

VM. You don't have to worry when things don't work. The number of times Casals said, 'No... No ... No ...' wasn't discouraging or depressing at all, because (as I've had to say to pupils when they've said, 'But there's *so* much that you've asked me to throw out . . .') you know that if you're looking for *gold*, you're going to have a great big mullock heap you have to throw out for a saucer of, or a pinch of, pure gold, aren't you?

JA. Yes!

VM. So you don't have to regard your failed shots as 'failures'—they're just, as we glibly say, 'those mistakes that you learn so much from.' That's positive. You 'don't have to do *that* any more.' You 'won't have *that* again.' And when you get one you can keep, you say, 'Yes!' 'I'll *have* that!' And that's for your saucer.

So I think all those 'true successes' can only be reached from a state of greater integrity. And when you have a real success, that gives you that kind of . . . .

JA. . . . gold.

VM. Yes . . . gold . . . and pleasure of the kind I'd like people to be getting all the time. And perhaps we always need a little bit of miracle—there *must* have been, by chance, if not by design, a little bit of miracle for things to have come together for that to happen.

JA. Everything . . . comes together.

VM. Yes. And when I'm talking about your integrity of coordination, I'm talking about your attention being there at all levels.

JA. . . . your imagination.

VM. . . . your imagination being fired, yes . . . somewhere. And of course with the imagination being fired, and with pleasure coming along, one thing leads to another!

JA. Yes.

VM. And yet, it's all *work*. It's the only thing that's *really* work.

JA. And it's also a new discovering every time.

VM. Yes. Because you're never going to be the same tomorrow as you were today.

JA. No. So even just living from day to day, you can almost think, when you come to your practising, 'O.K. I've lived another day now, so I come to my practising today . . . '

VM. . . . as a different person!'

JA. '. . . and does my life experience in this past day bring with it to my playing . . . '

VM. Better not to wonder whether it does and to be looking just to see, but just to *know* that it must be so—whatever happened.

JA. Yes.

VM. And sometimes, of course, something's happened that has *dis*coordinated you, without your realising it. And so you don't have to worry too much about the days when it doesn't work, doesn't seem to work.

JA. Yes.

VM. But I think you should *aim* for one scrap of real . . .

JA. . . . gold.

VM. Yes . . . and pure pleasure, every time you practise.

JA. And if you *do* find that gold, then the chance *it* has to reflect back its wonder on your life . . . is phenomenal.

VM. Yes. If you're coming out of the practice room having had a bit of pure delight, rather than just having done your hour and a half of scales, wouldn't you be a different person?

JA. Ha, ha!

VM. There used to be an advertisement for Reckitts Bath Cubes, with a picture of poor old Lizzie as she treks along to the bathroom with her dressing gown trailing on the floor and with her towel over her arm, and then another picture as 'Lady Elizabeth Lavinia Montague Cholmondeley-Whatsit' as she comes *out,* and she's all beaming and sparkling, and everything has miraculously been ironed and pressed, and her hair's in order—*just* through one Reckitts Bath Cube!

JA & VM. Ha, ha ha!

APPENDIX:

THE ALEXANDER TECHNIQUE
AND THE PROFESSIONAL MUSICIAN[1]

BY VIVIEN MACKIE

If we look at the development of music over the last few hundred years we see a remarkable process at work. We see the makers of instruments devising finer strings, better reeds, more efficient fingering systems, and the players exploring the new possibilities; we see composers, inspired by the finer instruments and by outstanding performers, extending their own boundaries, and writing ever more challenging music. We see the less

---

[1] Abridged from an article published in *Interlude, Journal of the Boston Musicians' Association*, Local 9-535, July-August, 1990.

remarkable players catching up with yesterday's best, and so on and on. Standards and expectations have spiraled steadily upwards; as in sport, yesterday's record has become today's norm.

If we look at where this had led us, we see a marvelous abundance of fine players, but we also see a distressingly high proportion of musicians dropping out, at all stages of their professional lives, through what are described as 'musicians' injuries.' To deal with this problem, the number of 'musicians' clinics' is steadily rising, where musicians in trouble can be examined by a doctor and sent for treatment of one kind or another. Correspondingly, we see a great rise in the number of conferences and seminars dealing with musicians' stress. On medical advice, students are withdrawing from required performance exams in disturbingly large numbers.

Does this mean that we are approaching our physical limits? We know the pressures we are under as performers. What are these pressures doing to the way we function? Do we perhaps need to change the way we use ourselves? Is it *possible* to change the way in which we use ourselves? It certainly seems that we are not as good at managing our own bodies as we need to be.

Frederick Matthias Alexander was a performer in trouble. He was an actor, who was born in Tasmania in 1869. He was enjoying some success in Melbourne and Sydney when he began to suffer from increasing hoarseness, sometimes culminating in a complete loss of voice towards the end of a performance. He took the very normal step of consulting his doctor, to see whether the trouble could be explained by some abnormality in his throat. The doctor prescribed soothing pastilles and sprays, and when these proved ineffective, suggested that he rest his voice completely for a period of three weeks. This seemed at first to be the answer, but very soon the hoarseness returned as before. The rest had merely delayed the onset of the symptoms. The next step was to have his larynx examined by a specialist. The examination showed that his larynx was in perfect order. Alexander reasoned that if his larynx was in perfect order and yet not functioning adequately, he must in some way be misusing it. Accordingly he set to work to observe himself in a set of mirrors to see what he was doing amiss. Before long he saw that when he raised his voice, he pulled his head back, depressed his larynx and audibly sucked in air. Closer examination showed that this pattern was occurring even in his ordinary speech. He set out to eliminate these movements, and found that he could not do so. They appeared to be inseparable elements bound into his whole pattern of vocal use. As he says at this point in his account of his experiments, 'I found myself in a maze.'

Alexander's patient and lengthy experiments first bore fruit when he discovered that if he could maintain what he described as a 'lengthening of stature' while he spoke, the hoarseness simply did not occur. He found that, in order to maintain his 'lengthening of stature' he had to prevent the shortening of the neck muscles which resulted in the pulling back of the head. When he was able to inhibit this shortening, the depressing of the larynx and the sucking in of air did not happen. The head, then, was the key.

He was able to return to the stage, and the improvement in his performance was so striking that his colleagues were curious to know how it had come about. He showed them what he had discovered, using his hands to demonstrate the new head-neck-back relationship which brought about the lengthening of stature. To his surprise, he found that, far from being an idiosyncrasy of his own, the tendency to pull the head back was present in his colleagues also, and the lengthening of stature was as beneficial to them as to himself.

George Coghill, the American biologist, was an almost exact contemporary of Alexander. During the early part of the century, he was investigating the development of movement in primitive vertebrates, and his experiments showed that 'movement is controlled and integrated by the total pattern of the head, neck, and torso, which dominates the partial pattern of the limbs.'

At the University of Utrecht, meanwhile, Professor Rudolf Magnus was studying the head/neck reflexes in animals, and his conclusion was that 'the whole mechanism of the body acts in such a way that the head leads and the body follows.'

Here, then, were three men in their different fields and by their own methods, making the same discovery. But Alexander showed how the primary importance of the head-neck-torso relationship also applies to man, and can be put to practical use.

By 1912 Alexander was using the term 'Primary Control' to indicate the dynamic relationship of head, neck, and torso which brought about the 'lengthening of stature.' Later he was able to state that 'this Primary Control governs the working of all the mechanisms, and so renders the control of the complex human organism relatively easy.'

In the skills required to play a musical instrument we are obviously making very great demands on our coordination, and we need to have superb control. How can we make use of Alexander's discovery in this situation?

Alexander teachers can use their hands to help us to experience the new head/neck relationship which will initiate the lengthening process. For example, a teacher will ask a pupil to allow the head to release gently forward and up from the neck in response to his or her touch. Keeping a hand on the pupil's neck, the teacher will then ask the person to make some simple movement, such as moving an arm as if to draw a bow, while maintaining the lengthening direction. At this point the pupil is likely to shorten the neck muscles and so pull back the head. He or she must inhibit any immediate reaction to the instruction, which will be a habitual reaction, in order to include the lengthening element. If successful, the pupil will have carried out the two instructions simultaneously—namely, to move the arm and to maintain the lengthening. The movement made under the new conditions is likely to feel quite unfamiliar. As lessons progress, the pupil will become more skillful at inhibiting the habitual reactions in order to maintain the lengthening. The student will become more aware of the interference with the primary control, be able to tackle more complex movements, and so become progressively less dependent on the teacher's hands. Since *the neck is the starting point of the pattern of tension*, inhibition at this level will prevent the spread of tension to other parts of the body—the undesirable reactions will be nipped in the bud.

In 1976 Frank Pierce Jones described his studies of the 'startle reflex' with high-speed sequential photography. Using one of his students as a model, and a sudden loud noise as the stimulus, he showed how, in the startle reflex, the pattern of tension begins in the neck muscles and passes down the trunk and limbs in about half a second. If this response can be inhibited at neck level—that is, if we can prevent the shortening of the neck muscles—the pattern can proceed no further.

Any of us will be able to recall an experience of the startle reflex when we have had a fright. Along with the postural changes comes a sudden quickening of the heart rate, due to the release of adrenaline into the bloodstream, and perhaps a sudden chill, with sweating of the palms of the hands, etc. The autonomic nervous system is in fact preparing us for fight or flight.

All musicians are familiar with at least some of these symptoms, which we describe as 'concert nerves.' We are experiencing a mild form of the startle pattern, and we know how incapacitating it is. What we may not appreciate is that many of us are living more or less permanently in this altered state, which has become so habitual that we accept it as normal.

It is important for us to know that movements are made by contraction of muscle, and that the contraction is virtually instantaneous, whereas the decontraction, which restores the muscle to its normal resting length, takes about ten times as long. This means that movements performed repeatedly at very short interval—as in a trill, for instance—will involve a progressive shortening of the muscles concerned, since there simply is not time for full decontraction to take place. Each repeat of the movement therefore requires more contraction than the last. This also applies, on a grander scale, to a long bout of practice. (This is why it is important to take frequent breaks, so that the muscles we have been using can return to their resting length.) Unfortunately it is possible for a much-used muscle to 'forget' its resting length, and fail to decontract as fully as it should; so we may get a permanent shortening of certain muscle groups, which shows as round shoulders, when the chest is over-contracted for instance, or in hands which refuse to open fully. We shape ourselves by what we do.

Frequent or prolonged anxiety will impose its pattern by the same process. Furthermore, the anxiety pattern includes the chemical component; that is to say, the postural pattern itself makes us feel anxious. A vicious circle indeed.

With the use of the primary control, we have it in our power to match the response exactly to the stimulus, which means that we can choose our habits. As players of musical instruments, forming desirable habits, as well as discarding habits we do not want, is what practice is all about. How we practise becomes critical, and Alexander's work gives us a proper physiological basis for thinking about 'how.'

If we can deal with anxiety, and if we can choose our habits with precision, we can work with far greater refinement and economy. We may then find we have access to potential we always believed we had—potential which has been locked away beyond our reach. Is this possibility not something we must pursue for ourselves, for our pupils, and for those who will follow us in our profession?

ABOUT THE AUTHORS

Vivien Mackie, née Couling, was born in Edinburgh, Scotland, in 1931. She attended Cheltenham Ladies College and the Royal College of Music. In 1952 she went to Prades, France to study with Pablo Casals, initially for ten lessons; but she stayed on to continue her studies with him until 1955. With her late husband, the conductor Gordon Mackie, she had two sons, Andrew and James; and from 1970 to 1973 she trained as a teacher of the Alexander Technique with Walter Carrington. She lives in London and travels worldwide, teaching and giving classes for performers in her fusion of the principles of Casals' teaching with those of the Alexander Technique. From 1990 to 1993 she conducted a three-year teacher training course in the Alexander Technique exclusively for musicians in Melbourne, Australia.

Joe Armstrong trained as a teacher of the Alexander Technique from 1969 to 1972 with Walter Carrington. Since then he has specialized in teaching the Alexander Technique to professional musicians in Boston, also holding bachelor's and master's degrees in music as a flutist. He studied flute with Carl Petkoff, Alexander Murray, and Fernand Gillet, and served for three years in the U.S. Army Field Band. From 1976 to 1988 he ran an Alexander teacher training course, and in recent years he has written fairly extensively on both the Alexander Technique and music-related subjects.